This book is a true breakthrough for co-parents struggling to positively interact or who want to get it right from the beginning. I highly recommend it!
– JACK CANFIELD, Coauthor of the bestselling *Chicken Soup for the Soul*® series including *Chicken Soup for the Parent's Soul*

Couples who have experienced the trauma of divorce and are trying to co-parent their children in the best possible way, will find this book extremely helpful.
– GARY CHAPMAN, Ph.D., Author of *The 5 Love Languages*

... Recommended reading for any stepparent, divorced parent, or blended family member looking for guidelines and concrete steps for co-parenting success. Readers motivated to improve interactions and make better choices must add Combative to Collaborative *to their arsenal of positive change!*
– MIDWEST BOOK REVIEW

A must have guide for divorced parents and those parenting separately
– WILLIAM L. GEARY, Divorce Attorney

Teresa Harlow's book is like a vital GPS that guides couples in their separation and custody arrangements. Her practical tips are respectful reminders of not only the children's needs but those of both parents as well.
– SUSAN ZIMMERMAN, Author and Licensed Marriage and Family Therapist

Parents working together is always in the best interest of the family and Combative to Collaborative *should be required reading for all co-parents.*
– GLORIA REDDING, Author, Family & Education Life Consultant

In a world filled with so much conflict and division, it is refreshing to find a positive approach to what is often such a negative experience. Teresa Harlow does a good job reminding parents they are supposed to be the adults in the room.
– REBECCA L. PARKER, PH.D., Founder and Chief Collaboration Officer, Something To Say

As someone who experienced divorce, co-parenting and step-parenting, I highly recommend this book. It is straight talk for navigating the best outcome for the children involved.
– CINDY CIPRIANI, Success Coach, Author and Speaker

COMBATIVE
TO
COLLABORATIVE
THE CO-PARENTING CODE

• • •

TERESA HARLOW

PROMETHEAN PUBLISHING LLC

Printed in the United States of America
First Edition 2021

Library of Congress Control Number: 2021905085

Developmental Editor: Ellen Coleman
Copy and Proof Editor: Rachel Shuster
Cover Designer: Kay Collins
Interior Designer: Thomas Nery
Author Photo: Kiki Israel

ISBN-13: 978-1-7367611-4-4 (paperback)
ISBN-13: 978-1-7367611-0-6 (hardcover)

TABLE OF CONTENTS

INTRODUCTION

• • •

We've all seen the sad examples of kids devastated by their parents' separation. Maybe you were one of those kids.

Some parents use their kids as pawns to manipulate their co-parent. Others are so hurt that they set out to compete for favor with the kids; some even go so far as to alienate their child from the other parent.

Some children had to hear one parent bad-mouth the other without either parent considering their feelings. Some were victimized by stepparents.

When parents separate, it usually involves pain and anger between the two. They agonize over ending their relationship because they have children together, but they know there must be a happier life on the other side.

You may be contemplating ending a relationship right now. Maybe you separated recently or ended your relationship with your co-parent years ago.

You're likely reading this book for one of three reasons.

1. Co-parenting is new to you and you want to get it right.
2. Your current attempts to co-parent are NOT working.
3. You're doing OK but you think you and your co-parent could do better.

Whether you are newly separated, have been on your journey a while, or are struggling to even get on the same planet with your co-parent, *Combative to Collaborative* will help you chart a course to a better place.

To focus your energy on the concerns you're dealing with now, the book is divided into three stages:

STAGE 1: Uncoupling

STAGE 2: Life Goes On

STAGE 3: Correcting Course

I encourage you to read through the entire book from beginning to end at least once even if you are ten years into your co-parenting experience. "STAGE 1: Uncoupling" lays foundational principles that are helpful in all stages of your experience. And I don't want you to miss these valuable tidbits.

If you're new to co-parenting, you'll find that this book provides you with a plethora of ideas to consider and actions to take as you and your former partner establish your separate lives as co-parents. STAGE 1 will set you up for success, and STAGES 2 and 3 will keep you on the right track (or get you back on it) throughout your journey.

If your current attempts to co-parent are failing or have somehow gotten off-track, you're probably very frustrated and desperate for answers. Although I encourage you to start from the beginning, you may want to start with "STAGE 3: Correcting Course," and then double back to read STAGES 1 and 2. No matter how hopeless your situation may feel, there is always a way to improve your circumstances. And no matter how long or how far things have gone off course, it's never too late and there are always more options to try.

On the other hand, you may think you're doing an OK job as co-parents. You may even have thoughts like, "We're doing the best we can, *given* the circumstances," and, "We're getting through it." You may even have told others "We're just focused on putting the kids first. It's not about us." Really? You're now a martyr—a bystander to your own happiness? Couldn't you do better than just get through it? Somewhere inside, a nagging voice is telling you that you can do better. What you are doing is simply not as good as it could be.

The problem isn't that people don't put their kids first. They want their sons and daughters to be able to look back and say they had happy childhoods. The problem is that they fail to recognize that working together to co-parent their children and root for each other's success as parents benefits them and their kids. They fail to understand the full value of the effort to get everyone involved. People set the bar for successful co-parenting way too low.

This book will give you the motivation and the guidance you need to reach beyond "just getting through it." You *can* create those wonderful childhood memories. You can *save* your family! By adopting an empathetic mindset, following the Golden Rule, and making intentional choices, I achieved both of these things. And you can too!

* * *

My first book on co-parenting, *Happily Divorced*, is the story of how my son's father and I successfully co-parented our son. I wanted to go deeper with this book. Here I shine a spotlight on combative behaviors and their effects on both the children involved and the parenting efforts. My goal is that you will learn to recognize your own combative behaviors, understand the impact of them on your parenting efforts, and learn how to change your mindset from combative to collaborative.

For those on the receiving end of what feels like a constant firehose of combative behavior, I offer strategies for dealing with the negativity you are subjected to in more constructive ways. You will learn what you can do to defuse and even transform your co-parent's combative behaviors into more positive interactions.

In short, this book will help you and your family move from anger, animosity, and agitation to consideration, kindness, and cooperation.

In each chapter we'll focus on a particular issue and review common combative behaviors parents engage in. I share true co-parenting stories from my own life and experiences shared with me by others. Then I suggest DOs and DON'Ts to keep you aligned with collaborative behaviors. Finally, at the end of each chapter, I offer a list of questions and thoughts to help you view the situation from the perspective of the Golden Rule. This is what I call the *Co-parenting Code. Treat others—*particularly, in this case, your co-parent—*as you want to be treated.*

When you finish reading the book, if you're still not sure what to do to move the needle in your own relationship, I encourage you to take the next step and sign up for my free co-parenting blog at TeresaHarlow.com. If you want one-on-one help, consider my Co-parent Coaching program.

If this book helps you to improve your life and the lives of your family members, share it with others so that they too can benefit.

To be clear, this approach will not work for everyone. There are exceptions. For instance, I highly doubt that this approach will work where violent behavior of any sort exists between family members—either involving the couple or the children. I'm not talking about the uncharacteristic outbursts that take place at the onset of the divorce scenario, but rather, real violent behavior displayed by either spouse. Second, it is unlikely this will work if you don't share the same core moral values of the other parent. Sure, you can be mad at the other person, because you are hurt, he cheated on you, or she always put you down. These may only be symptoms of an unworkable living arrangement, but for this to work you should at least share a common definition of right and wrong.

If you are simply *unsure* about whether you meet this last prerequisite, I believe you probably can unless you *know* you can't. If the other parent stole from you, killed your pet, or beat you, this probably won't work for you. Otherwise, give it a shot.

Parenting is tough. Divorced parenting may be tougher. I'm not really sure. Being a single parent or remarried parent certainly complicates the already difficult task of raising a child. But to be clear, it is the most important contribution we can make to this world. Set up your child, yourself, and your co-parent for success. Commit to being a good parent and move from combative to collaborative behavior now!

To family and happiness always!

STAGE ONE

UNCOUPLING

1

WE HAVE TO TELL THE KIDS

So here you are. You told your spouse or significant partner you're through. Or maybe, they unexpectedly pulled the rug out from under you. You've probably cried and cursed. You may have even left your home to seek sanctuary somewhere else. It's only a matter of time before you have to tell the kids.

Oh damn! What will we tell the kids? What if he tells them first? What if they overheard us yelling about it? We've got to get on top of this quick. Should we do it together? Can we do it together? What if the kids cry?

Dear God, we're about to change the rest of their lives! If they don't handle this well—if we don't get this right—they could end up as one of those sad statistics that say children from broken families are doomed to fail at love, their careers, and basically life in general. So let's get this straight. We're not about to change their lives. We're about to potentially ruin them. No pressure.

COMBATIVE APPROACH

Lots of parents screw this part up. They share all the nasty reasons why they are splitting with the kids. "Your dad's a lazy bum." "Your mom is a whore." "Your daddy is in love with someone else."

Maybe it all goes down at the same time. You ask for a divorce. Your spouse flies off the handle and in fear of your own safety or maybe losing your kids forever, you abruptly grab them up, run out the door, and tell them you're all leaving forever.

Some of the worst examples I've heard are, "Mom doesn't want to live with us anymore," and the equally painful, "Daddy doesn't love us anymore."

Now, you're probably thinking, "Geez. I'm not stupid. I know better than to do any of these." But there are more subtle ways to screw this up that are also damaging not only to your kids but to your future relationship with your co-parent. Let's face it. Unless you really are planning to abandon your children, when you have kids with someone, you are inextricably tied to this other human at least until the children are grown. Among the bad choices are:

- Telling your child without the other parent present.
- Telling the kids when you're in a fit of anger.
- Implying that the kids were any part of the decision. Like, "Dad wants more freedom," or "Mom wants to focus on her career."
- Leaving stuff out. Even more subtle but still damaging, are the things you don't say, which leave room for the kids to fill in the blanks. Things like:
  - "I just need to find myself."
  - "Dad doesn't want to live here anymore."
  - "Mom is very angry right now."

By not specifying the object of the other parent's angst, the children may assume that somehow, they are to blame. These feelings can linger throughout their lives, leaving them with immense feelings of guilt for what they perceive to be their role in ruining the family.

If your co-parent goes down one of these combative paths, I'd encourage you to initiate a private conversation with them. Ask them to commit with you to focus on being good parents. Assure them that you are going to put all of your effort there to make sure that the children you share together have the support they deserve to thrive.

> *By not specifying the object of the other parent's angst, the child may assume that somehow they are to blame.*

TRUE STORY

The following was contributed by my son, Ian who recounts the moment when at age five he was told that his father and I were divorcing...

I remember the day my parents told me they were getting a divorce. They were both sitting on the couch next to each other, crying, not necessarily holding each other. Through tears and deep, broken breaths, they explained to me what was going to happen.

I don't know how much I actually understood at the time, but I do remember walking outside by myself after my parents had finished detailing the situation. I was pointing at the ground, cursing the devil, saying it was his fault that my parents were getting a divorce. As I look back on that now, watching five-year-old me standing in the backyard blaming Lucifer for my parents' separation, I definitely chuckle—for many reasons.

13

I was under the impression that everything in my life was about to change dramatically and for the worst. While things did change A LOT, I cannot remember a time when my life was specifically bad as a result of my parents' divorce. I never felt the need to choose between one parent or the other; I never felt a competition between my parents for my affection; I never feared my family was going to disappear.

It can be hard to really analyze a situation when you are engulfed in it. Sometimes, an outside perspective or different point of view can really shed light on the unknown. Watching other friends' experiences with their intact families hitting full meltdown gave me this outside perspective. I watched their families turn from love to hate in a matter of months. I watched my friends struggle with the pressure of feeling like they had to choose one parent over the other knowing full well that whichever parent wasn't chosen would be heartbroken if not actually angry. That sounds like the most unfair, stressful thing to put anyone through, especially a child. I'm not sure how my parents did it, but they avoided all of these horrible situations that seem so stereotypical in divorced families. I always felt equal love from both of my parents and still do to this day, and I share the exact same, in return.

COLLABORATIVE APPROACH

If you're not ready to ruin your child's life and saddle them with a future filled with guilt, anger, and sadness, you're in luck. You don't have to. By using the following steps, you can make sure your child, regardless of their age, is left understanding that this isn't their fault or because of them. You can let them know that it is OK to be angry or sad. You can assure them that, while their lives will change, you will always be there for them, you love them, and you will do everything in your power to reduce the impact on them.

- **DO** tell them together—unless there is a history or real risk of physical violence. Look, you've been with your partner this long. You can stand a few more minutes. Your kids have earned that from both of you. It need not be a long conversation.
- **DO** choose a time when you're both calm.
- **DON'T** wait until they figure it out on their own. They WILL resent this.
- **DON'T** give detailed reasons why the two of you don't want to be together anymore. All you need to say is, "Your mom (dad) and I have decided to not live together anymore." If your children ask why, simply say that that is between the two of you and has nothing to do with them.
- **DO** tell your kids it is NOT their fault and that they did not do anything wrong, nor did they cause this.
- **DO** tell your kids that you both love them.
- **DO** tell your kids that you will both still be there for them always (assuming this is the plan).
- **DO** let your kids know it is OK to feel sad or even angry but assure them you will work to minimize the impact on their lives.
- **DO** listen to your kids and ask them how they are feeling.
- **DO** be prepared to answer questions like, "Who will I live with?" or, "Where will I live?" DON'T panic if you haven't figured these details out yet. You can simply say that you are working through that and assure them that as soon as you know, you will share the details with them.

- **DON'T** sit silently while the other parent does all the talking. This will leave your kids wondering if you agree with what is being said.

- **DON'T** be tempted to go back to your kids afterward and fill in more details about the reasons for the split. While this may feel cathartic to you, it will only hurt them and set up future problems. Either you will make them feel angry toward their other parent or you might unwittingly make them question whether they too have something inherently wrong with them. If you think making them angry at their mom is maybe a good thing, because after all you think she's a piece of shit, be careful. You do want her to be able to effectively parent your child. Don't handicap the other parent from doing this by imposing your opinion on your children.

- **DON'T** pile on with more combative behavior, even if Dad is antagonistic. Meeting him on his level will do nothing to make your situation better.

THE CO-PARENTING CODE

When planning how you will break this news to your kids, you need to step outside yourself for a few minutes and consider four things.

- How will it sound and feel to your child?
- How will it sound and feel to your former partner?
- Will you be setting yourselves up for a combative or collaborative relationship going forward?
- Will you be setting your child's other parent up to be an effective parent?

2

WHO "GETS" THE KIDS?

* * *

One of the most important decisions you'll make early on as co-parents is how you will split your time with your child. This can be painful for you as you consider the moments you'll miss with them. You may start visualizing nights alone in your house or not being there to see your child wake up Christmas morning. Or you may be freaking out as you consider having your children all day every day while holding down a fulltime job and maintaining a household by yourself.

OK, I get it. You're wallowing in self-pity right now. But snap out of it! Statistics show that children do a lot better in all aspects of their lives when both parents play an active role. There is a lot at stake for them. According to the Centers for Disease Control (CDC), the overall divorce rate has declined slightly over the past decade. Still, 50 percent of children in the U.S. will witness the ending of their parents' marriage. Ninety percent of moms are granted primary custody of the children—meaning the fathers are granted either some or maybe even no *visitation*—or as I like to call it, parenting time. With this, 43 percent of children in the U.S. are being raised without their fathers. And 60 percent of people below the U.S. poverty guidelines are divorced women and children. A full 65 percent of divorced mothers receive no child support whatsoever.[1]

So, let's talk about how your child's time will be divided between you. Then in the next chapter, we'll cover where everyone lives.

As you contemplate parenting time, it is important to not only consider the child but also your mental and emotional health. Can you be apart from your child for long stretches of time and still function? Can they be apart from you? If not, then get creative and design a schedule that will ensure everyone's mental and emotional stability. In the spirit of the Golden Rule, you should also consider how your co-parent may cope with being separated from their child. If you're not sure, ask.

If your child is older, say middle school or high school age, they'll probably have some opinions on the topic, and whether you decide to do exactly what they want, they will feel more respected if you listen to what is important to them and acknowledge their desires. They are hurting too!

When it comes to legal custody arrangements, there are basically two options:

• Sole Custody
• Joint Custody

---

[1] Jane Anderson, "The Impact of Family Structure on the Health of Children: Effects of Divorce," *The Linacre Quarterly*, National Institute of Health (November 2014), 81(4): 378-387; https://www.ncbi.nlm.nih.gov/pmc/articles/PMC4240051/.

Then within these, visitation schedules can vary depending on what the parents want and what's in the best interest of the child. Common arrangements include:

- 50/50 shared parenting or some other breakdown.
- Standard visitation where kids stay primarily with one parent and the other parent gets the kids every other weekend and one evening per week.
- Only supervised visits or no visitation at all in cases where there are concerns for the child's safety or well-being. Courts sometimes impose these restrictions if a parent has a history of domestic violence, substance abuse, or other destructive behaviors.

COMBATIVE APPROACH

Suing for Sole Custody

If you want to start a fight, tell your co-parent that they'll never see their kids again. Or threaten to sue them for sole custody. If there is truly a danger to your child by spending time with the other parent, this may be your best and only choice. But for most, this isn't the reality. Instead, it translates to parents spending a ton of money on lawyers and court fees, leaving less for both to provide for the kids going forward. And to what end? Denying the other parent and the child the right to have a relationship? Is this in anyone's best interest?

If you are being sued for sole custody, engage the counsel of a family lawyer.

Disregarding Your Ex's Parental Rights

I personally know three moms who picked up and moved with their children out of state without notice to the father.

They unilaterally banished these children's fathers from their lives. In two of these cases, private investigators were hired and tracked down the moms and kids. The fathers had to then go through the court system to force these moms to return to their home state to honor their custody agreements. And this is no small matter. Refusing to do so puts the parent at risk of being found in contempt of court and subject to fines or even jail time. A parent can even be charged with kidnapping or abduction in some circumstances.

In these scenarios, the moms simply chose to disregard the rights of the fathers and their children to take part in each other's lives. There's a term for those who go down this path. Well, there are many terms but the one I'm referring to is the psychology term referred to as Parental Alienation Syndrome (PAS). To be clear, there are both mothers and fathers who carry out this cruel behavior. As if the parent and child being separated from one another isn't bad enough, the damage doesn't stop there. In many of these cases, the child also suffers the loss of connections with grandparents and other extended family with whom, until that point, they may have enjoyed cherished relationships. Imagine a child's grief when not only does a parent disappear from their life, but also cousins with whom they played and grandparents with whom they cuddled.

If you are being alienated from your child and efforts to resolve matters directly with your co-parent have failed repeatedly, seek the help of a family lawyer. You may have to hire a private investigator or file charges. A family lawyer can advise you on your options based on local laws.

Insisting on or Conceding to Unequal Parenting Time
There are less drastic measures that some parents take which are also not ideal for the child—such as insisting that the

standard visitation schedule observed by many states be adopted. Unfortunately, this is still the most common arrangement co-parents choose. My guess is because it is easier than doing the hard work to sit down together, actually having to communicate, and coming up with a better plan. The standard schedule works like this: The mother is granted full custody of the children with the father getting *visitation* every other weekend and Wednesday evening from 6-9 p.m.

Is it just me or does the word *visitation* piss you off too? It is so negative, evoking visions of prisons or hospitals. It is not an appropriate term to associate with the hopefully happy time a father spends with his children. And the allowance of time? How many parents—particularly fathers— lack a consistent connection with their kids when so little time is spent with them? Forced to pack all that life offers into a mere fifty-three hours every two weeks, it's no wonder they don't want to spend a minute of it imposing discipline.

> *If your child's other parent suggests a more restrictive schedule than you would like, stand up for yourself and voice your desire.*

If your child's other parent suggests a more restrictive schedule than you would like, stand up for yourself and voice your desire.

Making the Child Choose

Another misstep some parents make is putting the burden of choice on the child. Asking a child to choose between their parents is at worst parental manipulation, and at best a parent who has abandoned their adult responsibility, unfairly shifting this extremely painful decision to the child. You can ask the child if they have a particular expectation, but you shouldn't ask them to tell you how much time they want to spend with each of you.

Still, while there is a common misconception that once a child reaches twelve or thirteen years old they "get" to decide which parent they live with or spend time with, this is not entirely correct. Where the courts are involved, while many judges will consider the child's wishes, the parents typically maintain control over the parenting schedule and living conditions.

Of course, if a teen adamantly refuses to go to the other parent's house, few courts will force them to go. This is one of the reasons it is important for both parents to establish a strong and ongoing relationship with their child. By doing this, the child will consider the parent's part in their lives as essential, expected, and beneficial to them.

Failing to Maintain a Consistent Schedule

When an equitable schedule is established, many parents don't honor it consistently for one reason or another. There's the dad who says he can't take the kids this weekend because he has to work or the mom who refuses to let the kids go to Dad's for the weekend because she has scheduled them to go to birthday parties, a weekend camp, or some other activity she lined up without considering the parenting schedule. Of course, sometimes, special occasions will arise and there should be a level of flexibility afforded. But this should be the rare exception. There needs to be a sincere commitment from both parents to make it a priority to maintain the schedule when at all possible. Parents should discuss any exceptions and reach agreement on schedule changes in advance.

A consistent schedule is comforting to a child. Don't you take comfort in knowing where you'll be sleeping tomorrow night? Imagine this being up for question. Such uncertainty in a child's life can be a great source of anxiety. Strive to provide them stability and predictability around which they can plan, dream, and prosper.

If your co-parent is not keeping up their end of the deal, talk to them to try to find out what is going on. Do they understand the schedule? Do they understand how important maintaining the schedule is to the child and to building a collaborative relationship with you? Do they have issues with the schedule or taking the child during the times agreed? Seek first to understand before chalking up their behavior to being irresponsible or not caring about their children.

Disallowing Access to the Child When with the Other Parent

I want to pose a question as we start down this path. Does your child stop being your child when they aren't at your house? Of course not. No matter where our children go in life—even if we leave them—they are still our children, and we are still their parents. For this reason, parents should do their best to afford a co-parent reasonable access to the child at all times. These days, cell phones are a great tool for achieving this goal.

Escaping Domestic Violence

Of course, there are extreme cases involving risk to the child's safety where sole custody with one parent, supervised visits, or moving away with the kids may be the safest option. If you are in this situation, seek legal advice, protection, and support. There are a host of charitable organizations available to assist those escaping domestic violence including the National Coalition Against Domestic Violence (ncadv.org) and the Domestic Violence Hotline at 1-800-799-SAFE (7233). For other local resources, consult the local directory available from the United States Department of Justice Office on Violence Against Women (https://www.justice.gov/ovw/local-resources). It is in no one's interest for either you or your child to remain in an abusive situation.

If you are abusive or prone to violent behavior, the best thing you can do for yourself and your children is to seek help from mental health and/or medical professionals. Get counseling in anger management. Explore the root causes of your behavior with the help of a therapist. You *can* turn things around with help and by demonstrating that your behaviors have been rehabilitated. Do you want to be a good parent? Don't give up on yourself or your child. They are counting on you. By taking corrective measures, you may be able to regain your parental rights and restore your relationship with your children.

Abandoning Your Children

On the opposite end of the combative spectrum from parental alienation is parental abandonment. I highly doubt that anyone who has abandoned their spouse and children is reading this book. But if you are, I implore you to think about the long-term consequences to both the child and to you. Seek the help of professionals, a spiritual advisor, or trusted family or friend to help you gather your feelings and work toward a more productive and positive situation.

If your child's other parent abandons them, seek the help of mental health professionals and support organizations such as Big Brothers Big Sisters®. Above all else, assure them that you will not leave them and that it is not their fault that the other parent left.

TRUE STORY

A friend of mine, who was in a twelve-year-long custody battle with his daughter's mom, shared with me that he was never permitted to talk to his daughter on the phone at her mom's house. I asked why not, and he said the mom told him it wasn't his time with his daughter and that he would have to wait to speak to her during their visitation schedule. Damn...there's that word again.

Now, I could see if he were calling several times a day or calling at what was obviously inappropriate times. But what we're talking about here is a father's sincere attempt to stay connected to his child when he couldn't be with her. He didn't call too late or too early and wasn't really given a good reason for being denied. Unfortunately, these parents were following the standard visitation schedule which afforded the father and daughter precious little time together. Also, because these two had never been married, they didn't have a divorce settlement with a parenting plan to consult in such matters.

The mom in this example had unilaterally decided that this father shouldn't be in his daughter's life. Maybe she thought he was a bad influence. Maybe she didn't want the two to develop a bond because she was afraid the daughter would choose him over her. Or maybe she disliked him so much for her own reasons that she just didn't want him to be around either of them. What wasn't the mom thinking about?

- Her daughter's desire and need to have her father in her life.
- How she would feel if she were denied access to her daughter.

And what do you think the father did in response to this? At first, he did nothing and just missed out on having conversations with his daughter in between visits. But then he decided to act. No, he didn't attempt to have a rational conversation with his ex. She had not laid the foundation for collaborative communication nor accepted his attempts to do this. Instead, he set about solving this problem without her. He bought the daughter a separate cell phone to talk to him when she wasn't with him. In effect, he resorted to a covert measure and asked his daughter to participate in it. He told the daughter not to let her mom know she had it and warned that if she did, the mom would probably take it away. Great! Now the dad is encouraging his daughter to deceive her mom. And he's using fear to do it.

I understand the dad's frustration and the desperation he felt. Unfortunately, he didn't consider how he might feel if he told the mom not to do something and she did it anyway. He was too caught up in his anger about the denial and toward this woman to see things through her eyes. Also, he didn't consider that he was teaching his daughter that if someone tells you no, rather than trying to work it out honestly, go around them and take action you know they won't like anyway.

The mom was furious when she found the phone and of course took it from the daughter. Sure, this may have happened anyway had he simply discussed it with her. But I think it's a pretty sure bet that you will increase hostilities with someone if they say "no, I don't want you to do that" and you do it anyway.

Instead, he could have attempted rationalizing with her and express why it was important to him and their daughter that they talk on the phone between visits. If she still disagreed with letting them talk, he could have at least been honest and informed her that he was going to get her a separate phone as an alternative. He could have even invited her to let him know if any issues arose with the use of the phone. He didn't have to necessarily cave in to her will. But if he were going to do what she didn't want anyway, doing it secretly just made it ten times worse.

COLLABORATIVE APPROACH

Only you and your co-parent know your circumstances and can assess what's right for everyone involved. But I would encourage you to do something you probably didn't do very well toward the end of your relationship. Communicate. You need to talk about it.

- **DO** discuss with your co-parent what you each want and what you feel is best for your child.

- **DO** consider your career schedules, how far apart you will be living from one another, your child's schedule including any activities they are involved with. Then review possible arrangements to decide what works best.

- **DO** listen to your child but DON'T ask them to decide how much time they will spend with each of you. This is painfully unfair to them. Instead, pose open-ended questions to them to get them talking. For example, say, "Your dad and I have talked and we're thinking we'll be splitting our parenting schedule with you 50/50. You'll be with one of us one week, and the other the next. How does that feel to you?" Just remember, the final decision of parenting time—that is, outside of a full-on refusal to comply from a headstrong child—rests with the parents even when the children are teenagers.

- **DON'T** use others as your excuse for not maintaining your parenting schedule. You are not at the mercy of other people's schedules. Put in the effort to condition those closest to you and your child to think about your parenting schedule when making plans. Still, there will be times when you simply can't work it out and you or your child will miss something that you really wanted to be part of. This is an unavoidable consequence of joint custody. But take peace in knowing that in the bigger picture, sharing custody is absolutely in the best interest of your child.

- **DO** consider everyone's emotional health. Is one of you likely to suffer severe separation anxiety? If so, devise a strategy to minimize the emotional toll such as:
  - doing a midweek swap during a week-on/week-off schedule
  - daily video calls with the child
  - serving as the before or after school option when the other parent isn't available
  - providing transportation to sports or other extra-curricular activities on your off-week
  - Participate in school volunteer opportunities that lead to you spending time with your child during the school day.
- **DO** be consistent while allowing for some flexibility. On the hopefully rare occasions where you ask to modify the schedule, reciprocate the time and this courtesy if requested. In other words, if you receive extra time with your daughter, offer Dad additional time during his next turn with her. If you gave up time, offer to take your child an additional amount to make up for it, but don't expect it. If you don't like giving up the time with your child, say no to things that interrupt your parenting schedule or find ways to accommodate them inside your existing schedule.
- **DO** hold each other accountable and ask questions of the other parent to determine causes if they fail to hold up their end of the bargain.

THE CO-PARENTING CODE

As you contemplate the time you will spend with your child, you will undoubtedly feel the emotions very deeply. As you think about how this is affecting you, take time to remember that the other parent and your children are also experiencing emotional upheavals. They may be different from yours or they may express upheavals differently. But always work to incorporate empathy into your thoughts, words, and actions. Contemplate the following questions as you decide on your parenting schedule.

- Have I clearly communicated what I want and expect to my child's other parent?
- Have I listened to what my child's other parent wants and expects? Regardless of my feelings toward him or her, is what they want or expect reasonable for a parent to suggest? Regardless of my current feelings toward the other parent, can I reasonably accommodate their request without unfairly relinquishing my parenting time and influence?
- Have I listened to what my child wants and expects? As I listened did I mentally put myself in their shoes, thinking back to how I might have felt going through this at their age? Have I acknowledged their concerns, fears, losses, and anger?
- Have we set expectations of being consistent while allowing for some flexibility where special circumstances are concerned, noting that this should be the rare exception to the rule?
- Have we communicated our parenting schedule to others in our lives with whom we socialize so that it is considered when planning special events and gatherings?
- Have I visualized managing my emotional disappointment when the schedule prevents me from doing certain things?
- Do I have justified safety concerns with my child spending time with the other parent?

Notes

3

---/---

WHERE WILL EVERYONE LIVE?

. . .

Having already decided how your child's time will be split between the two of you, it's time to decide where everyone will live. The kids want to know, "Who will I live with?" and, "Where will we live?"

If location drives real estate value, I'd say proximity to the other parent drives co-parenting value. Think about it. If you've agreed to joint custody, one or both of you will be bringing the children to the other parent's house at least as frequently as your parenting schedule shifts—typically weekly. Then there are the occasions where the child leaves something at the other house that is needed for the week, the stuff they need that comes up midweek, and the desire to see either the other parent or other family and friends when absent from them. Add to that the school and extracurricular activities your children participate in and you'll end up with a rather lengthy list of occasions that will require transportation to and from each parent's home to the other.

In the last decade, parents have become increasingly creative in designing their post-divorce living arrangements. While it is still most common after a breakup for parents to establish two separate homes in which their children each live part-time, parents today are exercising some other choices. Common options include:

- One parent keeps the existing home and the other moves to a new residence
- Two new separate homes
- Alternating time in one home, known as "nesting" or "bird-nesting"
- Everyone lives together
- Next-door neighbors

Old Home/New Home

For some families, it is possible for one parent to keep the family home while the other parent moves to another location—either a second house or an apartment, depending on finances. Keeping the family home is a great choice if the parent retaining the home can afford it. However, if you were only able to afford a home because you had the financial backing of your partner, doing it without them is probably not realistic. Even if they have agreed to pay alimony or some other money toward your family home, this may not actually happen.

Remember the earlier statistic citing that 65 percent of divorced mothers receive no child support? This isn't necessarily because the courts didn't order it to be paid. Unfortunately, there are situations in which the payment simply isn't honored. It could come about because of sheer negligence of the other parent or it could be that they've experienced an income reduction due to a hardship such as job loss or illness. My advice would be to retain the old home only if one of you can do it without assistance from the other parent, or anyone else for that matter.

Also remember you may have to buy your partner's equity in the home. This reason alone disqualifies many as it means coughing up the cash or financing the extra and driving up the mortgage payment.

Of course, real estate is about location, location, location. If you are in a highly desirable location with great schools, close to extended family or friends, or the home has other valuable attributes that are difficult for you to recreate in a new home, it may be worth it to make concessions so that the finances work. You may have to sacrifice some extras like trips or new cars. But if you can make the budget work, consider whether it is worth it to allow your children to stay put.

On the other hand, do you look around your family home and continuously recall all the bad things that happened there? Would you like the opportunity to start fresh and leave all that negative history behind? Now's your chance. Just remember that depending on your state's laws and individual financial circumstances, if you sell your existing home, you may each be entitled to half of the proceeds. Check with your attorney and accountant. Then plan accordingly for the available funds you'll need toward a new place.

Two New, Separate Homes

One of the most common choices parents make is to sell the family home, split the proceeds, and both parents establish new separate households in other homes. If you go this route, I highly recommend you set a maximum distance from which you and your co-parent can live from one another. Put this in your divorce and/or custody agreement. Some parents agree to reside within the same school district, which allows for a variety of added conveniences including being close for school functions and, in some cases, bus transportation.

> *In your custody agreement, set a maximum distance you and your co-parent can live from one another.*

In my case, we established a forty-five-mile parameter. However, when it came to choosing specific homes, we ended up living within one-half mile of each other.

Of all the choices that made life easier and better when we divorced, I would have to say that living this close was it. In the True Story section later within this chapter, I elaborate on the many benefits we gained from this one decision.

Of course, just as with all other options, carefully plan how much you can afford to pay for your new home considering all the changes in your financial picture.

Nesting or Bird-nesting

In this modern arrangement, there is one primary residence where the children live full-time. The parents then take turns rotating in and out of the home on a routine schedule. When not in the family home, the parents may choose to share an apartment or second home that they rotate in and out of. For those with the financial means, both parents may acquire separate homes to live in when not in the family residence. Still others may have a separate apartment with one or more roommates which they live in during their "off" week.

From what I've observed and from my own experience having "bird-nested" for about four months during the early days of our separation, this is usually done on a short-term basis. We did it while we prepared to sell our joint home. It served very well in the short term to relieve the tension that comes from cohabitating with someone from whom you are divorcing. The negative energy when together can be overwhelming, and it can feel like you're watching your marriage die. This negative energy can also affect the kids. Although you should consider timing any residential moves to minimize disruptions to school and extracurricular schedules.

When implemented as a short-term fix, you can also consider temporary housing options such as living part-time with a family member or friend. Since you won't actually be taking your child to the other residence, many of those close to you could be willing candidates.

If you're considering bird-nesting for your permanent plan, you and the other parent should set ground rules around housekeeping, visitors, and household expenses. Can you both agree not to bring other romantic interests to the family home? If you are sharing a parent residence that you each rotate in and out of, be sure to cover the same bases for that home.

Everyone in One Home

Yes, some people even do this! Personally, I don't know how. But if it works for them, more power to them. We see this choice made more frequently when there is something going on economically that prevents the equitable sale of the family house. In 2009, there was a severe downturn in the price of homes, and many found themselves owing more on the house than they could sell it for. As a result, rather than taking the loss and not having any money to pay toward new homes, many parents stayed put until home prices rebounded.

In 2020, many parents stayed put in the same home due to the COVID-19 global pandemic. With health concerns and aggressive restrictions on movement from place to place coupled with a severe shortage of homes for sale (no one was moving anywhere), it just wasn't tenable to make a move to separate homes until things rebounded.

2009 and 2020 were extraordinary circumstances. However, in "normal" times, continuing to live together will probably only work for a small number of parents or for a short time. After all, it would be difficult at best to realize most of the *gains* from divorcing. Starting fresh, making your own independent choices, eliminating the conflicts caused by living together, and eventually moving on to new relationships are all pretty difficult if you still live under the same roof.

Sure, everyone living together in one home is the most attractive choice financially and maybe for the kids too if conflicts are kept to a minimum. Just be aware that once either of you begins to explore new romantic relationships, the other will have a bird's-eye view of these activities. That could become extremely awkward if not troublesome.

Become Next-door Neighbors

In a variation on the two-home concept and bird-nesting options comes a compromise—co-parents living next-door to one another. These include:

- Single-family homes next-door to or across the street from one another
- Twin singles or duplexes
- Adjacent town homes or condominiums
- Adjoining apartments

Frankly, I wish we had thought of this when we divorced twenty years ago. If you can stand the idea of being able to see each other's comings and goings, AND be good neighbors to one another, this is certainly a great choice for the kids, imposing a minimal disruption on their family unit.

COMBATIVE APPROACH

At the onset of a divorce announcement or breakup, emotions run hot, and fear of the unknown is palpable. Yesterday you knew what tomorrow would look like—or at least you thought you did. Then WHAM! Everything is changing and nothing is guaranteed about tomorrow. In these moments you become vulnerable to overreacting, making bad decisions, falling prey to vengeance, and judging situations too rashly. For these reasons, you must find a way to defuse emotions so that you can think rationally about what is best for everyone in the long term. Below are some examples of decisions parents make that set up a combative relationship.

Refusing to Leave

For many reasons, a parent may refuse to leave the family home. They may fear if they leave their kids behind, they'll never see them again. They may believe that if they leave the home, they are relinquishing their residential status. In some cases, these two concerns are real. If you have these concerns, you should definitely seek legal advice.

But some people going through a breakup have more malign motivations for refusing to leave. And this, my friends, is truly the best way to lay a foundation for a combative relationship with an ex. If you are refusing to leave just out of spite or to make life more difficult for the person you are breaking up with, this behavior will be returned to you. Has everyone met my friend *Karma*?

If your co-parent is refusing to leave, you can call the cops to ask them to remove the ex. But until there is a legal separation agreement or physical harm inflicted on you, they cannot force a legal resident of the home to leave. They, like you, can only suggest it. Now all you've accomplished is pissing off your former partner by calling the cops on them. So why involve them?

Further, the sight of cops at and in your home can traumatize your kids and even you. It's not because police are bad—on the contrary, they are a great help and are experts in defusing domestic disputes. They do it all the time! Yet their presence is still intimidating by design. The flashing lights, sirens, uniforms, and deadly weapons strapped to their hips are designed to intimidate us so that we heed their direction in times of chaos. This intimidation coupled with the unknowns your children are already dealing with can add to their fears that bad things are going to happen to them and those they love. They may think that one of you is going to get arrested. They may incorrectly conclude that one of you has broken the law.

I'm not saying there aren't appropriate times to involve the authorities. Certainly, if you fear for your or your child's safety, you should call 911 immediately. Heightened emotions can cause otherwise rational humans to be unpredictable and make poor choices. What I am saying is that if you are involving the cops because you think they can make your ex-partner leave, they can't. Instead, your best choices are to:

- Calmly reassure the other parent that you will not use their leaving to stake claim to either the kids or the property.
- Go to separate areas of the home removed from one another and minimize interactions within the home until a more permanent solution is reached.
- Get on with the legal separation.

Refusing to Sell the Home and Split the Proceeds

I get it. You or your ex-partner may be very fond of your current home. Maybe the idea of losing it is simply more than one of you thinks they can bear when so much else is going wrong. Maybe you think if you refuse to sell, you can force a reconciliation—that the other parent will cave financially and agree to make it work. Or maybe you just want to make life as difficult as possible for all they are putting you through. The problem is no one can move on. Not you. Not your ex. And not your kids. You're just prolonging the pain for everyone.

If your co-parent won't leave the family home or agree to sell, ask them if they are prepared to buy your equity. If they are not, remind them that if they are not willing or able to pay your equity, then they are just prolonging the inevitable and preventing everyone from healing. You might want to encourage them to talk to a divorce attorney to understand their options better.

Living Long Distances from One Another

A friend of mine had to drive hours each way to trade the kids with the co-parent. And this made it far more difficult to attend school functions and, depending on the location, other activities in which the child was involved.

Then there are the parents who take job transfers to other states, making anything other than long absences between one parent and the child all but inevitable. Would you want the other parent to live so far away that it would place a burden on you to accommodate their parental rights?

If you are the custodial parent and contemplating a move that takes you a great distance from the other parent, I want you to consider something. How would you feel if the shoe were on the other foot? What if they up and moved a hundred or even a thousand miles away with your child in the pursuit of a career or love interest? Wouldn't you feel that this completely disregarded your and your child's relationship?

Again, I strongly encourage you to set a maximum residential distance allowance in your parenting agreement to guard against such moves.

Preventing the Child from Taking Things Between Homes

This one kills me. Some parents are so possessive of the stuff they buy their kids that they won't allow them to take clothes, toys, or anything else with them to their other parent's home. And I'm not talking about family heirlooms, just the basics. Maybe it's because they've done so in the past and nothing ever comes back. While I get it that you don't want to constantly be buying new clothes, it's upsetting to your child if they can't take a favorite T-shirt or stuffed animal with them to their dad's place. Is it really worth that? Further, Mom shouldn't have to fear that if she lets little Joe take his trumpet with him to Dad's to practice over the weekend, it will never return.

One guy I dated had to buy new clothes every other weekend for his daughter as Mom wouldn't send any with her or return any that the daughter wore home from Dad's. He was constantly without clothes for the second and third days of her visit and ended up buying new clothes constantly. Eventually, he got sick of doing this and made the daughter change out of whatever he had bought her back into what she had worn from her mom's. This child must have thought that her parents were either very immature, crazy, or both! Then again, without knowing any better, she may have concluded that this was acceptable behavior.

There was even a point at which this father bought the daughter the guitar she wanted for Christmas. When it was time to return to Mom's house, the daughter wanted to take the guitar with her to practice during the week. Mom refused to let her play it when at her house. Exactly what point was she making? Did this show any empathy for her daughter's feelings? Did it somehow serve her interests? I guess she thought she was *getting back at* the father for past transgressions. In reality, she was just pissing him off while denying her daughter something she really wanted that he was able and happy to provide. But at least she got her way, right?

If you and your co-parent are quarreling about these things, maybe it's time to recommit to being good parents and putting your focus on that effort rather than on each other. Even if your ex seems unwilling, put it out there anyway. Tell them that you want to spend your time and energy on being a good parent rather than on fighting about clothing and physical items. Ask them for help in solving the problem. Say something like, "How can we get past our differences and focus on giving (child's name) what (he/she) needs?"

Disregarding Wildly Unequal Incomes and Home Lives

You are not responsible for your ex-partner's level of earnings or lifestyle. Nor are you obligated to match theirs. Still, if there are big differences in income, your child is probably going to have a vastly different experience at each home. While she enjoys a pool, lavish décor, and off-the-chain entertainment options at your place, is it OK if she's living in a homeless shelter when she's with her mom? I know this is an extreme example. But it does happen. And even a less dramatic gap can pose problems.

I'm not suggesting that a co-parent is legally required to supplement the ex's income if it hasn't been ordered by a divorce settlement. But before fighting against and resenting paying child support, consider that this is a way to even out the living conditions. Another strategy for balancing the experience at both homes is to allow the child to take some things back and forth between homes and buying duplicates of special items to keep at each house.

Of course, there are parents that don't use the child support to pay for things for the kids at all. Instead, they use the money to fund a breast augmentation or buy a new car for themselves. While this too is selfish and combative behavior, don't use the other parent's bad choices as justification to deny paying child support. This only make matters worse for the child.

If your home is not as extravagant as the other parent's, beware of the desire to keep up. I'm not suggesting you shouldn't be driven to improve your circumstances. But don't do it to compete with them. Instead, do it because you want those things for you and your child. If your former partner works eighty hours a week, leaving no time for the children, and you have a modest home with a lot of time for them, who's really better off? However, if your circumstances are desperate, such as facing homelessness or living in a dangerous neighborhood, have a conversation with your ex to air your concerns and see if they can help you come up with a plan that gets not only you but your shared children into better living conditions.

TRUE STORY

When my son's dad and I decided to separate, there was the immediate need to relieve the tension that comes from cohabitating with someone from whom you are divorcing. But as neither of us could afford to just take time off from work to sort through it all, we had to come up with another interim solution. We ended up splitting weeks in the house. One week I would stay there with our son and Bob would stay with family. The next week Bob would stay in the house with our son, and I would go to my girlfriend's house and stay in her guest room. We didn't know it at the time, but this short-term arrangement is what is now referred to as bird-nesting, which I explained earlier in the chapter.

We talked about what to do with our home, and ultimately, we concluded that neither of us could afford it alone as we were a two-income household by necessity. So we sold it and divided the proceeds. Selling it was hard since we had only built the place two years earlier. I loved that house. But in the end, it was better to leave behind the negative energy we had deposited there as we started our new lives.

At this point, I looked at many neighborhoods, many homes, and a couple of other school districts. Fortunately, we were both able to fund separate homes. While we would both have to downgrade on the luxuries slightly and not have as much money left over for extras, we could provide a comfortable home—actually two—for our son.

I wanted to stay in the exceptional school district we were in and got lucky enough to find another home that I could afford in the same neighborhood on a street with several boys my son's age. While the home was smaller, the lot backed up to a beautiful natural setting which felt like an upgrade to me, something that eased my pain of losing our other home.

My son's father built a home that was in an up-and-coming neighborhood through a thin line of trees and across one main road directly behind my house. It was only about a quarter mile as the crow flies which I knew meant that as our son got older, he'd eventually be able to walk or ride his bike between our two homes.

Something I didn't think about as much was how living so close made so many things easier on all of us. Since we were in the same school district, there were some years when my son could take the bus from and to either his dad's or my home. And when that wasn't the case, his dad was so close, he could drop him off to me in the morning since he worked earlier, and I could put him on the bus. This gave me a chance each day to see my son before school. Then there was the ongoing transfer of clothes, toys, sports equipment, homework, and music instruments in between homes.

When our son was young, I or his father packed his stuff up. As he got older, he started doing it himself. Over the years, whether it was us or him, hundreds of items were left and had to be retrieved from one house or the other. We both got frustrated from time to time with this but acknowledged that it couldn't be easy living in two places at once. I had never done it and was sure if I had, I'd have been running back and forth in between houses daily if not hourly to get a particular jacket, book, or stuffed animal.

To minimize some of the running back and forth, we bought duplicates of some of the main items. If you can make this happen with the items that your child uses most often, it will really relieve your stress. We also used this strategy to offer roughly the same experience at each home. We even bought our son the same bed. As much as we had competed during our marriage to win every conversation, neither of us was interested in seeing the other one lose in the parenting game. We had finally found a motivation to be nice to one another.

In our case, we purchased two swing sets, two bikes, plenty of clothes for both houses, and two drum kits. Oh, there had to be two drum kits! It was a sizable investment and we each had to make some sacrifices to make it happen. But it was so worth it. Otherwise, one of us would have never seen our child or we would have been stuck carting that set back and forth for years to come.

When our son reached adolescence, we realized other benefits to living close by. Since there was only one house blocking my view of his dad's backyard from my back door, I was comfortable allowing our child to walk between our homes. I could watch him walk most of the way and his dad could see him on the other side when I lost sight. This was very handy not only when items were forgotten at the other home but also worked out quite well during the middle school years when he hung out more with the kids on his dad's street than on mine. This was great. I never wanted him to prefer one home over another because of our choices. And I never wanted him to be bummed out that he had to go to another home and leave his friends behind for a week. Oh sure, there was some of this, especially when our inter-district boundaries were different and the kids in the other neighborhood ended up at a different middle school and high school. In general, though, I think this arrangement's benefits went a long way to improve the circumstances of our separated family. But it didn't happen by accident. We chose to make it happen this way.

To be clear, you have choices regardless of how much money you each make. It may mean offering or receiving more child support to make your co-parenting living conditions ideal for everyone. But those are available choices. If your co-parent is not offering child support to make up for an income discrepancy, talk to a family lawyer or research the matter online. Most states have a formula which accounts for these disparities. You can try applying this formula to your situation and then sit down with your co-parent to discuss how you can work together to give your child comfortable living conditions at both homes.

COLLABORATIVE APPROACH

Here are my recommendations for collaborating where residential choices are concerned.

- **DO** agree on a maximum distance you can live from one another until the children have graduated high school and put it in your divorce/custody agreement. I know this can be career-limiting for some. You may have to curtail upward mobility and the financial gains that come with it until your child is older. But the benefits to your family are immense.

  Of course, you may not feel that you have to establish a legal commitment to distance parameters now. But if your child is young, so much can change. And you don't want such an important matter to be left entirely to the idea that you will always have a positive relationship with your spouse. You never know who might influence your co-parent or you in the future.

  The legal agreement provides the other parent with some leverage or possibly even recourse should things change down the road. Parents are then compelled to weigh such decisions against possible legal penalties.

- **DO** try to stay in the same school district so that both parents can feel more connected to their child's academic community. Additionally, paying taxes to the school district where the child attends does make a parent feel more vested in the decisions of the institution.

- **DO** grant each other access to your homes, if you trust one another. This may sound crazy to some of you but there are a number of benefits to giving them this, either with a key or using a keypad. Of course, you have to have a high level of trust in them to literally give them the keys to your home, and it isn't for everyone. But if your only hesitation isn't a trust issue but rather an unnecessary belief "people just don't do that," then you're making life harder on yourself and your child for no good reason. Some might also say that you could deal with the issue by giving the child the access. However, let's be real. If the child has the key or code, then your co-parent has it too. Going further, if the other parent is forbidden from accessing the other parent's home and the child is young, the other parent will be handicapped from helping them should they need help in any way.

- **DO** allow the child's clothes, toys, and other reasonable items to be transferred between homes and talk about this expectation with your co-parent.

- **DON'T** hold items sent to your house with your child hostage. Be considerate and make sure they go back with the child or at least confirm whether they need to go back with the other parent.

- **DO** work to minimize inequities between homes.

- **DO** meet each other halfway or trade off on the commute if you must live a great distance from each other, so that the burden is shared between both parents.

- **DO** be forthcoming and have a conversation with your co-parent if your circumstances change, putting your previous distance agreement in jeopardy. It shows you are considering them as you determine your options.

For example, if you get offered a promotion that requires you to move to another state, ask your co-parent if they would consider moving as well. If this is a no go, see if you can commute between cities or work remotely in the new role. Again, creative problem solving may be required. Or you may simply have to refuse the offer in the best interest of your family. You need to weigh the costs and benefits.

THE CO-PARENTING CODE

Life is about choices. You have a particularly important one to make in this regard. To help guide your conversation and decisions around your living arrangements, consider the following questions:

- What is the maximum distance you want to commute between homes until your child has graduated from high school?
- How close will you and your co-parent live to one another?
- Do you want your child to remain in their current school district? If not, what other options are desirable to you both?
- Which parent is designated as the residential parent for school districting purposes?
- What type of housing can you each afford?
- What items will you each provide for your children at your home?
- If living separately, what items do you expect to go back and forth between homes?
- Which living arrangement are you planning for the two of you and the children?
- How will you work together to make your child's living conditions relatively consistent at each home? Ask each other, "What do you want our children's home to provide?"
- Are you prepared to refuse favorable career choices in order to honor your maximum distance agreement? Where does the other parent stand on this?

4

SUPPORTING YOUR CHILD'S EDUCATION TOGETHER

* * *

Don't let your child become an academic statistic. Many studies have shown that children of divorce often earn lower grades than their peers whose parents are still together.[2] This is particularly true when the divorce comes as a surprise to them or when the parents become less involved in their schooling after a separation.

However, there are exceptions to this premise. For instance, if the family who lives together is high conflict, the child can actually fare better once removed from the volatile situation. Also, if a child can sense that a divorce is coming, they may be relieved when it finally happens.

The onset of divorce is certainly disruptive. Your child's usual schedule, living space, and family routines are suddenly all in question. As such, it is no wonder children lose focus during divorce. So do their parents.

---

[2] Jennie E. Brand, Ravaris Moore, Xi Song X, Yu Xie, "Why Does Parental Divorce Lower Children's Educational Attainment? A Causal Mediation Analysis," *Sociological Science* 6 (Apr. 16, 2019): 264-292; https://sociologicalscience.com/articles-v6-11-264/.

But there are many things you can do and avoid doing to encourage your children's continued academic success. Let's look at some of the combative behaviors that parents engage in which can undo their children's ability to be successful in school following a parental split.

COMBATIVE APPROACH

Unfortunately, some parents will drop the ball when it comes to their children's education following a divorce.

Checking Out on Education

When parents are going through divorce or a breakup, they are distracted, emotionally distraught, and consumed by their own concerns. For some parents it is just too much, and they can't or don't step back from their own problems to ensure their child is still fully engaged in school. Some parental activities from which parents disengage include:

- Not making sure their child's homework is completed
- Failing to attend curriculum night or teacher conferences
- Allowing the child to skip school for emotional health reasons
- Taking the child out of school when moving households or to attend court hearings
- Failing to monitor their children's grades or intervene if grades slip
- Not asking their child about their school activities
- Forgoing school performances, parties, and sporting events
- Stepping back from school parent volunteer activities
- Not telling their child's teacher what is going on with the family

Checking out on your children's academic concerns sends the message that it isn't a priority. As such, the child may likewise deprioritize schoolwork and academic success. This will undoubtedly reduce their future potential, if not derail it.

Withholding Information from the Other Parent

Some parents are more comfortable being in complete control and shut the other parent out intentionally from information about their child's education. Some avoid these communications for fear they will turn negative, accusative, or just plain uncomfortable. Others simply don't think about it.

Schools are beginning to recognize that all parents do not live together and are doing more to accommodate the needs of parents and children living in two homes. Some school systems now provide communication to both parents. But this is not always the case. When a school doesn't provide dual communication for parents who live separately, the residential parent (the parent of record according to the school system) is the only one who receives information. As such, it will be up to them to ensure the other parent gets this information. The nonresidential parent could miss out on:

- Report cards
- Test scores
- Disciplinary notices
- Attendance records
- School schedules
- School photo purchasing
- Sports schedules including tryouts and equipment needs
- Special events
- Volunteer opportunities which allow parents to be more involved with the school

- Academic and other school-related matters, especially when your child may be having problems. Wouldn't you rather have help?

Parents need to ask how they expect the other parent to effectively support their child's education without this information. Moreover, the custodial parent should consider how they might feel if they missed out on opportunities such as attending a special performance or buying school pictures. In fact, do they really want their child to endure the sadness of the other parent being absent from their special performances?

I'm sure some moms or dads don't bother to provide this information citing that their ex has never bothered in the past anyway. Maybe this is true. But enabling them doesn't help anyone. In fact, it just shifts the blame to the parent who failed to offer the information. Could the other parent seek it out from the school? Sure. But we are dealing with a government entity here and they're not exactly positioned for flexibility. Wouldn't it just be easier and in everyone's best interest to offer to the other parent all of the available information? If at that point the other checks out, this matter should be addressed separately and directly with them. But at least you won't be their excuse. Remove that obstacle for them and for your child.

Leaving it All to the Other Parent

On the flip side of the coin, we have the parent who chooses to leave all the school stuff to the other parent. This could be because they think since they're not the "custodial" parent, they are relieved of this responsibility. Maybe the other parent always handled school matters when they were together. Or it's possible they hated school and just don't take an interest in it.

Leaving it all to the other parent is in fact combative whether intentional or unintentional as one parent is choosing to burden the other with sole responsibility of matters that should be shared by both. If you are new to dealing with your children's school issues, consider the following:

- Now that you're no longer in the same household, you won't come about this information organically—by overhearing it, looking over your child's or partner's shoulder at school items. You have to replace these opportunities with intentional effort on your part. You must fill the communication gap yourself.

- As I stated earlier, checking out on your children's education sends the message that it isn't a priority. As such, the child may likewise deprioritize schoolwork and academic success. This will undoubtedly reduce their potential, if not derail it.

- The other parent's time is now divided just as yours is. They may not be able to cover everything as thoroughly as needed. Your child's education is a joint responsibility

> *Your child's education is a joint responsibility regardless of how much time you spend with your kids.*

regardless of how much time you spend with your kids. No one is going to let you off the hook later if your child fails in school. They'll still say it was both parents' (plural) fault. In fact, they may blame the absent parent more. "Yep, their mother, Jane, did all she could but their dad, Jack, never bothered when it came to anything regarding the kids' schooling."

- If you disengage from your child's school concerns, you won't be able to spot red flags which may tip you off to the onset of emotional problems, learning disabilities, physical difficulties, or psychological struggles. You also won't have a good grasp on the other adults influencing your child and molding their view of the world.
- You will miss a golden opportunity to demonstrate that you are still there for your child.
- You will be reinforcing to both your co-parent and school officials that you do not need to be considered. As a result, you will get less and less information about your child's school activities. This will be no one's fault but yours.

Failing to Provide Academic Financial Support

Some parents who are not designated as the custodial parent refuse to pay a penny more than ordered through the courts as part of their child support agreement.

But there are many related expenses that may not be covered by this calculated amount. To start, the residential parent may live at a particular address so that their child can attend school in a good school system. And to do so, they may pay a premium for their property. The nonresidential parent could choose to live outside the district to forgo this additional expense.

If your child attends private school, there's tuition and possibly uniforms. Then there are the lab fees, book fees, test fees, pay-to-play fees, extracurricular uniforms, lunch fees, school party expenses, field trips, and that long list of yearly school supplies. And let's not forget the enormous cost associated with college.

If your co-parent asks for help paying for these items, at least consider whether they are being reasonable. Also consider the benefits of these items to your child. If your ex has to do without to take care of these items and you don't sacrifice anything, are you really being fair to them or your child?

TRUE STORY

I remember the first night conference during which we met Ian's kindergarten teacher. We had separated about six weeks before. Of course, we both wanted to be there. So, we did this crazy thing: we talked about it. Then we did another crazy thing. We agreed to both go and let the teacher know that even though we were divorcing, we weren't one of those dysfunctional couples who hate each other and yell all the time, which was a kind of an interesting development since one of the reasons we split up was because of our incessant arguing. Yep, divorce, or at least living separately, seemed to fix our most outward dysfunction as a couple. Oh, the irony!

As we squeezed ourselves into tiny little kindergartener desks, I made my pronouncement to the new teacher, Mrs. Joseph, that we were divorcing but that we get along, and she would not have any problems with us. As it turned out, this was Mrs. Joseph's first year teaching *anywhere*. She was probably simultaneously concerned, skeptical, and relieved.

Ian had this teacher for two years, and as we approached the end of the second year, Mrs. Joseph, disbelieving or not, pulled me aside to tell me not only how special our little boy is (yep, Mom already knows that), but also how lucky he is to have two parents who work so hard to make this whole divorce thing into as positive an experience as possible for him. Now, those two words—*divorce* and *positive*—don't normally appear in the same sentence. But two years into our positive co-parenting approach and people around us were beginning to see the effect it was having on our son. And he was feeling it too!

COLLABORATIVE APPROACH

Most parents want their children to succeed in school. And sure, some care about education more than others. Whether you are considered the primary parent by the school and teachers or you aren't, if you want what's best for your child, you must do what is necessary to support your child's education.

- **DO** remain or become actively involved with your child's education after you separate from the other parent.
- **DO** let both school administrators and teachers know if you and the other parent are divorced or separated and if the child spends time living at each home.
- **DO** ask school administrators and teachers if they can send all communications to both parents.
  - If not, and you are the primary parent, DO make arrangements to provide the other parent with everything you receive.
  - If not, and you are not the primary parent, DO ask the other parent to provide this information to you.
- **DO** stay on top of things with your child. Ask them about homework, tests, school relationships, what they are struggling with, and those things that they find exciting.
- **DO** attend your child's school events as much as possible. If you can stomach it, sit with your co-parent and use it as an opportunity to bond over the common interest you share in your child.
- **DO** participate in volunteer opportunities when possible. This will strengthen your bond with the school community, other parents, and your children.

- **DON'T** expect your child to provide their other parent with school information.
- **DON'T** leave everything to the other parent just because they handled all educational matters when you were together.
- **DO** talk to the other parent if you notice warning signs pointing to physical, emotional, mental, or behavioral concerns with your child. With the two of you working together, you can both share the burden and contribute to helping solve whatever problems your child may be facing.
- **DO** reinforce the importance of education to your child to make sure they know you consider it a priority.
- **DO** discuss school-related expenses and how they will be covered between you. Be sure to include in the conversation how unexpected school expenses will be handled. What communication is expected? How will the cost be split? How will it all be tracked?
- If you are not the primary parent contact with the school, **DO** talk to school administrators, teachers, counselors, and your child's other parent to establish plans for them to provide you with all information pertaining to your child's education.

THE CO-PARENTING CODE

As you consider how to collaborate on education with your co-parent, here are some questions to keep your behavior aligned to the Golden Rule.

- How can you best support your child's academic success?
- How can you help your child's other parent support your child's academic success?
- How can you best enlist the help of educators in supporting your co-parenting circumstance?
- Do you consider your co-parent an ally in your child's education?
- Know that it is far more likely that your child will consider their education a priority if you do. They follow your lead and model your behaviors. Have you told your child how important their education is to you?

5

WHAT HAPPENS TO THE IN-LAWS?

* * *

Some people like their in-laws. Some hate them. And some simply tolerate them. When you split up, you have to face at what level the relationship with your child's other family will survive.

If you aren't very close or weren't together long, it will be easy for you to disconnect from your former spouse's extended family and vice versa. If you didn't like each other, you may use the split as an excuse to eject them or they you from each other's lives. If you liked your in-laws, you will be grief-stricken and may wonder if these dear family members are lost from you forever.

Or maybe your in-laws were part of your support system. They may provide you childcare, friendship, employment, or even a roof over your head. Depending on your situation, the answer to the question, "What is at stake?" could vary significantly.

But one thing we must remember is that these people are *your children's family* regardless of whether you stay with the other parent or wish a relationship with them after the breakup.

Extended family can play important roles in your children's lives. A grandparent may be a child's cuddle buddy, fishing partner, spiritual guide, life teacher, or mentor. Aunts, uncles, and cousins serve as playmates, trusted friends, and shoulders to cry on. And of course, they too could serve as role models to your children.

If you want these important relationships to survive your split with their family member, it will take intention, good communication, and consideration. Without these elements, you could end up living out one of the combative scenarios below.

COMBATIVE APPROACH

Denying In-laws Access to Your Children

Some parents—particularly those who harbor a lot of anger toward their ex or just don't like their in-laws—deny these extended family members contact with their children after a split. Grandparents and grandchildren become estranged from one another and miss out on this incredibly special relationship.

If you are not allowing your children to see your co-parent's family members, stop to consider how you'd feel if your children weren't able to see your parents or family.

If your former partner refuses to allow your family members to see your children, first look at what you can do to solve the problem on your end. Are you providing time for your kids to spend with your family when they are with you? Is your family asking because there is a special occasion? Have you asked them to honor your parenting schedule and plan events they want your children to attend during times when they are scheduled to be with you? Of course, sometimes this isn't possible. Maybe a particular event is only available on dates the children are with the other parent. In these cases, you'll need to appeal to your co-parent for an exception. But just as you would not want them asking you to give up your parenting time on a regular basis, don't expect it of them.

If your co-parent is still unwilling to let your children participate in special events with your family, talk to them about it. But rather than coming at them with accusations like "Why are you so difficult?" start by assuming that the behavior is unintentional and ask your co-parent for help planning for each occasion as it comes up. Give plenty of advanced notice and provide specifics regarding the event so that they understand the circumstances you are working with. This is simply a discussion between two parents. It need not be confrontational. If your co-parent raises issues, then work to find a compromise or some other creative solution that everyone can agree to.

In-Laws Cut Off Ties with You

Some in-laws cut off ties with the parent who is no longer with their family member. In doing so, they cut off many ties to the children involved and as a result become much less involved with them. This could be because of you or it may be that they are assuming you want nothing to do with them.

In this situation, initiate a conversation with your in-laws. Let them know that you would like to maintain a relationship with them and ask them if they would also like that. Let them know that you will make every effort to not talk about their family member so that they can relax knowing you're not planning to put them in the middle of things with the two of you. I know this could change over time. But at least start here. If they have been hurt or feel their child has been hurt and feel the hurt was caused by you, offer an apology for their anguish. Something like, "I'm really sorry. I know this has been difficult for you. I don't wish to cause you any pain."

In-laws Fail to Include Your Children

Is it combative behavior for your in-laws to fail to include your children in family gatherings? I suppose it's possible that they do this intentionally. But it could just be that they simply haven't figured out how to navigate the new version of your relationship to them. They may not be aware of the schedule. And if you haven't talked to them directly, they may not know where you stand or if you still want them in your lives. Your ex may not be good at communicating either to you or them, in which case plans simply don't come to fruition.

In this case, you got it. Talk to them. Let them know the kids' schedule and ask them to include your kids in extended family gatherings whenever possible. Also let them know that you too will try to be flexible so that the kids can participate.

Parents Fail to Put in the Effort to Sustain In-law Relationships

Some parents simply don't put in the effort they should to ensure children's relationships with extended family members survive the parental breakup. They don't nurture communication between their child and the extended family. They fail to have their child recognize family members' birthdays or allow their children to participate in special occasions with extended family even when it is during their scheduled time.

Putting Your Ex Down to Your In-laws

Do I really need to elaborate on this? I know you may want to justify your breakup or make sure that family members know it wasn't all your fault. You may have this desire to set the record straight. While some claims made by an ex to their family may warrant your clarification or correction, this is the exception. In most cases, you are better off to avoid discussing your co-parenting relationship with their family.

Even if you trust your in-laws deeply, the temptation for them to share with their family member whatever you say about them may be too great. They may even view it as a family obligation to do so. Be careful not to use them to do this either. It's not their affair. Don't saddle them with your dirty work. If you have something to say to your co-parent, pony up and tell them yourself. If you can't do that, maybe it shouldn't be said.

TRUE STORY

I have lived in Ohio, over 1,200 miles away from my parents, since my early adult years. This distance has denied me the simple pleasures of enjoying casual family dinners, playing cards, or just having a cup of coffee together on a cold winter weekend morning.

When I met my former mother-in-law, I felt an instant connection with her. She shared many admirable traits with my mom—solid values, unwavering honesty, refreshing authenticity, and a mother's protective attitude toward her children, which she extended without hesitation to me. My son's father and I frequently joined his mother and step-dad for dinner, holidays, and other family gatherings both planned and spontaneous. And it never felt forced or awkward with the exception of the many times we arrived after we had fought in the car on the entire drive to their house.

My sister-in-law was still in high school when her brother and I first started dating. Through the years, my sister-in-law and I shared many lovely memories. We laughed and cried together. We traveled together. She lived with us while she attended college, broke up with boyfriends, and then eventually met and married the love of her life. In fact, she and I were so close that I was the matron of honor in her wedding. This meant a lot to me. Of course, I thought I had ruined that friendship forever when only a month after her wedding, I announced my separation from her brother.

When I decided to divorce my son's dad, I was terrified of losing the relationships with his family. What would become of me? They were the ones I celebrated most holidays and special occasions with. They shared in our joy as we watched our son eat his first birthday cake, collect Easter eggs for the first time, and beat on his first drum kit. They were my local support in times of crisis or despair. Who would be that support now? I lived five states away from the only family with whom I communicated other than my in-laws.

When we divorced, I suddenly viewed myself as an intruder on their family. I felt I had let everyone down. They were devastated by our breakup. I really thought it would just be too hard for them to remain in my life. I certainly wouldn't expect them to betray their son and brother for my sake. Didn't associating with me mean they would have to do just that? Or did it? Would my son's dad find it in his heart and everyone's best interest to give his family *permission* to allow a continued relationship with me? I don't know how those conversations might have gone, but somehow, through all of the hurt and pain, my in-laws chose to keep both my son and me in their lives.

When we divorced, I suddenly viewed myself as an intruder on their family.

After we separated, my in-laws, including aunts and cousins, followed the lead of my son's dad and treated Ian with the love they had always showed him and continued to include me in their lives. When our son was young, I tried diligently to keep them apprised of significant events in his life so they wouldn't miss out on anything and he wouldn't miss them being there. When I needed a babysitter, I asked them first. And when I picked him up, we often still enjoyed that cup of coffee together. We shared pictures. We attended family gatherings together. When extended family attended our son's soccer games, school concerts, or other activities, I would always sit with them, and, in fact, save them seats. I felt no need or desire to separate myself from them. It seemed so much more natural to be with them. It wasn't me and them. It was us—my son's whole family!

My mother-in-law and I continue our relationship to this day. We send each other birthday and Christmas cards, talk on the phone, and have dinner together on occasion. I've shared in the difficult times with many of them too. It's just what people who care about each other do. And why on Earth should I not care about my son's grandmother, grandfather, aunt, uncle, or cousins? Why do I need to stop caring about them? I didn't divorce them.

I'm very thankful that my in-laws have remained in my life and that I can still call them my family too!

COLLABORATIVE APPROACH

There is a range of strategies you can employ to extend the relationship with in-laws beyond the end of your romantic relationship with their family member. There's also a lot you can do to keep them in the lives of your children. Here are some ideas for starters:

- **DO** allow your child to see their grandparents, aunts, and uncles.
- **DO** put in the effort to maintain a connection between your child and extended family members. Have your children call their grandparents regularly. Take them to visit.

- **DO** talk to your in-laws to invite them to remain in your children's lives and yours (if that is what you want).

- **DO** provide your in-laws with information such as sports schedules, performances, and your child's holiday and birthday wish lists.

- **DO** invite the in-laws to your home for family gatherings with your child.

- **DO** provide reasonable flexibility that allows your child to partake in gatherings and special occasions with their other parent's family.

- **DO** tell your co-parent that you would like to continue a relationship with their family. While you don't need their permission to do this, getting their buy-in will position things more comfortably for everyone involved.

THE CO-PARENTING CODE

To ensure you are honoring the Golden Rule when it comes to your child's relationship with the in-laws, consider the following.

- Does your child have close relationships with your co-parent's family that they will miss if no longer there?

- What level of connection do you expect your children to maintain with your family? Have you considered that your co-parent may want the same thing for his family and children?

- Do you consider your in-laws to still be part of your child's family?

- Do your in-laws still consider the children part of their family? Are you sure?

6

RECONCILIATION

Most children harbor a fantasy of their parents getting back together after a breakup. Remember the Disney movie *The Parent Trap*? Sure, there are kids that endured such combative environments when their parents were together that they have no desire to go back there. But most would still prefer to be in a home where both parents live together.

As a divorced or separated parent, you may be shocked to discover that what looked like green grass from a distance doesn't seem so green now that you're up close. Maybe you miss your former partner, your family, your old home, the way things were.

If you begin to question the entire idea of splitting up and find that your ex feels the same, you may consider reconciling. And I say full speed ahead. Give it your all! Just bear in mind that you've already put your kids through the breakup. They may already be starting to adjust to the idea that you live separately. Don't build up their hopes just to have to disappoint them again and set them back.

Many parents attempt reconciliation. Sometimes these attempts are successful and many times they fail.

Many parents attempt reconciliation. Sometimes these attempts are successful and many times they fail. But with a few considerations, it doesn't have to undo the progress you have made to establish a collaborative co-parenting relationship.

COMBATIVE APPROACH

Telling Your Kids Immediately

Telling your kids too soon that you and Daddy may get back together is very risky. If things don't work out, you'll be putting them through your breakup all over again.

Reverting to Poor Interactions with Each Other if Things Don't Work Out

Wow! Seriously? Didn't you already determine that working together on parenting was best for the kids? Is that no longer the case? Don't throw away the effort you've put in so far. You will still benefit from being able to positively interact as parents.

Holding a Failed Reconciliation Against the Other Parent

It takes two to tango. Holding anything against anyone frankly is wasted energy. Do you really have any to spare? What does it get you?

If things don't work out and your children are unaware of the reconciliation attempt, keep it that way. If your children were aware, there is no benefit to telling them too much about it. In fact, sharing this information can confuse and even anger them. They may start to question why you didn't try harder or place blame on one of you. Instead, use the same matter-of-fact caring approach you did when you told them you were breaking up the first time.

Consulting Your Children About Your Relationship with Their Other Parent

This may be tempting to you for many reasons. They know the other party. They care about you. They are right there. The problem is they obviously will struggle to remain objective. It's their parent you're talking about which will inevitably lead to them offering a biased opinion. And they have their own agenda which will be hard for them to keep out of it. Besides, it's not fair to involve them in your adult affairs. Even if you feel you have no one else to talk to and your kids are right there—your captive audience—you need to refrain from burdening them with these mature problems. As your kids become adults, there may be some validity to consulting them in such a case. But I would still proceed with caution and rather seek others to have this discussion.

Reconciling *Just* for the Kids

While admirable, without you personally having a desire to be with your partner, your efforts are likely doomed. Will you end up resenting your partner, your choice, and the additional time you invested?

TRUE STORIES

A friend I know married her high school sweetheart. They had a son together and then divorced when he was six years old. After being separated for about five months but still married, they decided to give it another go. They did not tell their son about it because they didn't want to get his hopes up in case their efforts failed.

After reuniting for one date, my friend realized that nothing had changed. The problems the two had were still there and she concluded that reconciling was not in the cards for them. The next day she told her co-parent that she wanted to finalize the divorce as soon as possible. The husband asked the wife if she was still going to co-parent with him and share custody. She replied simply, "Of course. We're not divorcing our son. We're divorcing each other." The son never knew they attempted reconciliation.

Compare this to another couple who decided to attempt reconciliation after being divorced for three years. Caught up in their excitement over the possibility of restoring their family, they immediately shared the reconciliation plan with the kids even as they planned their first evening together as a couple again. The children told their friends that Mom and Dad were getting back together and proceeded to adjust psychologically and emotionally to the idea of everyone living together happily in one home again very soon.

Unfortunately, two weeks into the reconciliation attempt, things fell apart and the couple decided to put the brakes on reconciling. They agreed to move forward as collaborative co-parents and broke the news to their three kids, ages eight through fourteen. The children were terribly disappointed, now faced with the embarrassment of having to go back to their friends and tell them the whole thing was off. They had to reset their expectations about where they would be living and relive much of the pain and disappointment they experienced only three years earlier.

This was particularly upsetting to the fourteen-year-old, who expressed his anger to his parents, telling them he wished he hadn't even been told they were thinking about it if they weren't sure. These parents should have taken a breath and considered waiting until they had tested the waters of reconciliation before getting their children excited about the possibility.

COLLABORATIVE APPROACH

If you do in fact contemplate or actually attempt reconciliation with your children's parent, keep the following in mind:

- **DON'T** tell your kids about reconciliation attempts unless or until you have decided to officially reunite. If you decide to move back under one roof, then it's time to tell the kids.

    If your co-parent tells the kids about your reconciliation attempt, they may have done so because they wanted to share positive news with them or because they are excited about the prospect of getting back together. DO acknowledge for your children that you two are working on things. Just be sure to minimize the information you share with them. Tell them you're taking it one step at a time, that nothing is guaranteed, and try not to make a big deal over it.

- **DO** agree that whether or not your reconciliation works out, you're both committed to remaining collaborative as parents.

- **DO** consider attempting reconciliation if you feel like you haven't tried everything. Otherwise, you may live with the nagging question of "what if" for the rest of your life. What's the worst thing that could happen? You end up no worse off than where you are now, and you will have gained assurance that you've made the right decision.

- **DO** commit yourself to the reconciliation effort but **DON'T** force it. If it simply doesn't feel right no matter what each of you does, you may be at the point where you simply have to accept that you must move on from your romantic relationship with one another to one based on your mutual goals as parents.

- **DON'T** confuse wanting to reconcile with your co-parent with wanting to restore the comfort of the known or avoid the fear of moving forward without them. Splitting up can be scary and riddled with many problems to solve. But getting back with them for any reason other than wanting or thinking you want to spend your life with them will simply delay the inevitable and result in a setback for everyone when the reunion ultimately fails.

- **DON'T** agree to reconcile because you feel guilty either toward your children or your co-parent about the breakup. Guilt alone is not a sustainable emotion on which to build a romantic relationship. It may work in the short term. But again, you may just delay the eventual breakup, give everyone false hope, and worst of all fail to be true to yourself.

THE CO-PARENTING CODE

●   ●   ●

To view the idea of reconciliation with your other parent through the lens of the Golden Rule, consider the following:

- Does your co-parent compare the end of your relationship with you pulling the rug out from underneath them? Even if you don't think this is the case, this is their perception. If you want to resolve such doubts, attempting to reconcile may provide both of you clarity.

- Do *you* feel satisfied that you did everything you could to save your relationship with your child's other parent? If not, exploring reconciliation may provide you with the peace you need regardless of how it turns out.

- If your reconciliation attempt fails, can your collaborative co-parenting relationship survive? Talk to your co-parent about this possibility and reaffirm your commitment to positive co-parenting regardless of the outcome.
- Can you each honestly tell your kids that you both did everything you could to stay together if they ever ask? If not and you still have feelings for one another or question whether you can revive those feelings, give it a try.
- Are you attempting reconciliation because you want to or because others want you to? Are you being honest with yourself? Are you holding your children and your co-parent back from creating a happier existence separately?
- Are you willing to forgive the past? If not, you or your partner will harbor resentment and lack trust in your relationship. If you decide to try again, start anew.

Notes

STAGE TWO

LIFE GOES ON

7

I'VE MET SOMEONE!

• • •

A failed marriage can really do a number on your ability to think objectively and rationally about new potential mates. Maybe you've spent years in a passionless relationship. You look around and all you see are happy couples holding hands, gazing into each other's eyes, and declaring their undying love for one another. You admire their joy, their happiness, and their acceptance of one another and wonder, "Am I even capable of that?" If others can be happy, why can't I?

When you're a parent, you may envision creating a new family for your kids. You want your children to see that love is still possible. You want to offer them the experience of a family where everyone lives happily under the same roof. You visualize family dinners, game night, picnics, trips, and Christmas morning. Never mind the fact that this new someone isn't their parent, and their actual parent is still in the picture.

You may seek financial security or a better life for your children by providing a two-income home. A better neighborhood, nicer house, money for your kid's college, those trips...all of that is far easier with the help of a second income.

Then someone—a complete stranger—looks at you with soft eyes. He laughs at your stupid jokes and tells you that you're perfect. And suddenly you are driven by desire to dive headlong back into the deep waters of romance. You ask yourself, "Is it too soon? Ah, what the heck—I've been unhappy long enough. And this will be a good thing for the kids too." We tell ourselves, "Sure, I failed in my last relationship, but I can still be swept off my feet. My child and I can still have our happily ever after. Let's do this!"

But if I can interrupt your newfound bliss for just a moment, what if your former lover is mortified by the thought of you being with someone else? Anyone else! While *you* may be ready to introduce the new boyfriend or girlfriend to everyone, *your ex* may not be ready to meet them.

In Chapter 9, I'll cover introducing the children to new people in your life. But first, let's review the many not-so-great ways in which you could handle introducing a new romantic partner to your co-parent.

COMBATIVE APPROACH

Putting Too Much Stock in a New Relationship Too Soon

Too soon is an ambiguous term. So how do you know if it's too soon to consider your relationship as serious? Well, how well do you know this person? Do they know you have kids? Do they want kids in their life? Do they even like kids? Have you assessed whether this person is financially stable?

Do they have any baggage? Kids of their own? A crazy ex? What about their mental and emotional health? Come on. Most people don't begin to show their true stripes until several months into a new relationship. Be careful not to be blinded by your fantasy of recreating your perfect life while missing the answers to all of these questions and more.

> *Most people don't begin to show their true stripes until several months into a new relationship.*

Telling Your Co-parent Too Soon

You have a handful of dates with a new guy, and you are completely convinced that the two of you are in love. You just want to get on with your fairy tale and get the awkward crap like telling your ex out of the way. Isn't that the right and honest thing to do anyway? You sure don't want them to come upon this knowledge through friends or by running into the two of you together somewhere. Certainly, telling them sooner rather than later is the best choice, right?

Of course, the other more devious motivation is that you want to throw your new relationship in your former partner's face at the first chance you get. "See, I am lovable! Look what you're missing out on. Ha! You're alone and I'm not. I win!"

Not so fast! First of all, did you get the answers to all the previous questions yet? How about this one…does this new someone agree that it's time to tell your co-parent? Have you asked them? What if their answer is, "Oh, well, I didn't think we were getting that serious"? Or worse yet, "About that…I'm married." Ugh, that would be super embarrassing if you've already told your child's other parent about them.

Not Telling Your Co-parent or Telling Them Too Late

Having your new romantic partner answer the door when Mom drops off the kids is a sure setup for combative reactions. Don't kid yourself into thinking they are going to be happy for you. Of course, maybe they will be. But they will not appreciate learning about it in this way.

That doesn't mean you have to tell them right away if you're not sure about this new person. But be thoughtful and use some common sense. Don't let your new romance answer your door.

Gushing When Telling Your Ex About Your New Partner

For real, this is even annoying to your friends, much less to your former lover. You may be thinking, "Duh! I'm not going to do that." But we've all had friends who drone on about how wonderful a new relationship is. If you're not careful, you could do this without thinking about it. And why is this a bad idea? Just think for a minute about how you would feel if this person with whom you used to share a life and had kids with starts telling you about how awesome their new mate is.

- Co-parent's translation option number 1—*"He's great and you suck!"* Not only is tearing down someone else's self-esteem mean, it doesn't contribute to a more cooperative relationship with them going forward.

- Translation option number 2—*My ex is trying to hurt me. So much for being nice to each other.* If your co-parent perceives that you are trying to hurt them, they will become defensive. It's human nature. They may in turn try to hurt you in some way.

- Translation option number 3—*I'm being replaced as a parent to my kids.* No, this isn't threatening to a parent at all. How does the idea of your kids calling someone else Mommy sit with *you?*

Introducing Your New Partner to the Children Before the Other Parent

This one may be controversial for some. But would you want to learn about your ex's new lover from your child? It just shows a lack of regard for the other parent. You introduced your child to a stranger without consulting their other parent. This could be perceived as reckless or at the very least, insensitive—not characteristics on which a foundation of collaboration is built.

Springing the News on Your Co-parent Publicly

Springing the news on your co-parent in public, in front of the kids, or with the new someone present is insensitive, risky, and awkward.

You may think you know the kind of reaction you're going to get to this news. But you cannot be certain of what your ex's emotional state is, how they personally have processed your split, or what crazy thoughts may be provoked by the idea of knowing you're sleeping with someone else. I don't care if you've been divorced for years, it may still feel like a stake being driven into their heart. Considering this lack of predictability, is it really a good idea to do this in front of others? Hell no. The public certainly doesn't need you adding such stress to their day and I'm really hoping you've taken my earlier advice and not told the kids yet. So, this would be news to them and not the best way to start things off with the new guy.

And speaking of the new guy or girl, I suppose you have them there for your emotional support. Terrible choice! Even if your co-parent fakes his or her way through the ordeal cordially, you've put them on the spot. Not a kind move. Just think about it in reverse. Still a good idea? Telling your former partner that you've met someone and introducing them should happen in two stages at distinctly different times.

TRUE STORY

A friend of mine shared that after she and her husband divorced, he quickly started dating another woman. A few months later, the two moved in together and then quickly married. The father then proceeded to insist that the kids, ages six and three, refer to this new wife as their mom. Not stepmom but mom.

How confusing this must have been for the little kids involved. Were they supposed to start calling their real mom something else? Was she going to go away? And how hurtful to the children's mother this must have been. I don't know that this father necessarily had bad intentions. But at the very least, he didn't consider how this one action would affect either his kids or the co-parenting relationship. This set up a terribly combative relationship between the mom and both the dad and stepmom—all at the cost of the kids and everyone else around them who had to endure many awkward encounters over the years.

COLLABORATIVE APPROACH

- **DO** consider first letting your co-parent know that you are dating again. You don't have to be specific; but this can give them a chance to start adjusting to the idea. It will then set the stage for the next level conversation about a specific someone if and when you get to that point.
- **DO** pause for a minute on the new relationship to consider whether you are happy with them or happy with the fantasy that the new love interest represents.
- **DON'T** tell your child's other parent about your new love interest if you're not sure about this new person. If

the two of you run into your child's other parent, just introduce them as a friend until you're ready to call them more than that.

- **DO** tell your co-parent about a new love interest *before* introducing them to your kids. Your children's other parent has earned this courtesy.

- **DO** tell your co-parent about a new love interest before you let them answer your door, answer your phone, or drive your car.

- **DO** tell your co-parent about your new mate before they move in with you, you move in with them, or you get married. Yeah, um...this is too late!

- **DO** consult your new partner about telling the co-parent. Do they have an ex to tell? The situations may be different and that's OK. But the two of you should at least agree that you are ready to take this step.

- **DO** tell your former partner about a new someone in a private setting without the kids or the new someone around. It could be on the phone. If the two of you don't talk at all, you could do it through email. Just be careful of what you put in writing. You could also have this conversation when you drop off or pick up the kids, assuming they won't hear or see your exchange.

- **DON'T** pull them aside where others can hear at a children's function to have this conversation. If there's no chance of a violent reaction or emotional outburst, you can pull them aside where others can't hear, but if there's any chance of violence or an emotional outburst, **DON'T** do it.

THE CO-PARENTING CODE

• • •

Just like all the other situations we've discussed so far, it's a matter of considering what you would want in this situation if you were on the other end of the equation and following that guide.

- Do you want to know if your children's other parent is dating again?
- When do you think they should tell you?
- How would you not want to learn about your co-parent's new relationship?
- What considerations would you like them to extend to you when telling you about their new someone? Extend the same courtesies to them.

8

I DON'T WANT TO MEET MY EX'S NEW "SOMEONE"

• • •

In the last chapter, we covered how to introduce your co-parent to a new love interest. Now let's flip script. What about when your co-parent wants you to meet their new romantic partner?

The experience of having your ex introduce his or her new love interest to you will probably feel a lot like a rerun from the moment one of you asked for a divorce. It's as if a stake is being driven through the heart of a once-promising relationship...ensuring it will never be brought back to life. You may be surprised that you feel this way even if you thought you had no feelings left for your former partner.

When a child is involved, it introduces an entirely new set of considerations. In Chapter 9, I'll focus on the introductions to the children. But first, in this chapter, we need to address the elephant in the room. Do you see it? It's the new girlfriend/boyfriend.

The reality is they are moving on whether you like it or not.

The idea of picturing your ex-lover being intimate with anyone else can be extremely upsetting. It may require you to cross a bridge you were dreading. Maybe you were holding on to some fantasy that someday you would get back together. Or maybe you wanted to be first so that you could prove to your ex once and for all that they really were the problem. But the reality is, you are separated and while you each may be in different stages of dealing with it, you can't control the other person's decisions. You couldn't when you were together, and you certainly can't now. So consult a therapist, meditate on it, or just face it. Have a good cry if you feel you need it. Then, recalibrate your romantic life, move on, and move on now.

The reality is they are moving on whether you like it or not. And yet the two of you will continue to be co-parents. You can't afford for this to ruin that relationship, even if it hurts right now.

In the best interest of your kids, and your own sanity, you need to find a positive way to process this revelation. You need to continue to communicate with one another and work together as co-parents. But how do you do this in a productive way that will serve everyone's best interest? For starters, let's look at what happens if you allow yourself to become confrontational.

COMBATIVE APPROACH

You're Told in Front of Others and Completely Lose it

Yep, this was an inconsiderate choice made by your co-parent. Apparently, they did NOT read my last chapter. So there you stand with others looking at you as you choke back tears or contemplate throat punching this person who just publicly embarrassed you. You want to cuss them out for telling you in front of others. But as my mom has always said, "Two wrongs don't make a right." If your co-parent makes a bad choice and you respond with another bad choice, now you just have two bad choices. When you react negatively, you actually amplify the negative situation—that is, you make it worse.

It may be hard but if you do feel yourself getting angry or emotional in that moment, take a deep breath, ask your co-parent if you can continue this conversation later, or politely excuse yourself for some made-up urgent matter. Then remove yourself from the situation until you can calm down.

You Express Your Congratulations to Your Ex but Then Bad-mouth Them to Friends and Family

Maybe you didn't like the way she told you, or you think the new woman dresses too risqué. You really don't understand what your co-parent sees in this new person and you share that opinion with friends and family. Now, you've not only amplified the negativity from the announcement experience, but you've also set the stage for future negativity. Your friends and family will judge your co-parent and this person harshly in support of you. They may even validate your negative commentaries by adding their own to them. Again, we're adding negatives.

You Bad-mouth the New Someone to the Kids

This can backfire in a few ways. The kids could tell their other parent. Now you're outed as a gossiper and have damaged your trust with them. Going further, if either your co-parent or the kids share your opinions with the new partner, now you have two people mad at you. This just keeps getting better, doesn't it?

Your kids may feel obligated to follow your lead or risk losing favor with you. Soon they're telling you unseemly stories about the new girlfriend or boyfriend that totally piss you off. Meanwhile, your children are making life a living hell for their other parent and the new person in their life.

Or they may like the new person. Maybe they're a positive influence on your kids. You could have another parent in your corner if you don't alienate them. Plus, now your kids have to feel uncomfortable about liking them and no longer feel free to share stories from their other home because it might upset you. Geez, who's putting whose best interest first?

The New Love *Is* Bad News and You Must Say Something

You see it. Everyone sees it except your co-parent. So you plan to sit him down for an intervention and tell him what's wrong with this new someone.

Oh, this is going to go well. Look, it sounds like you have good intentions. But unless you suspect your children are in real danger, you need to sit this one out. Leave intervention duties to someone else. Stay close to this new person and your co-parent so that you can keep an eye on the situation.

Instead of confronting them with accusations about the new guy or gal, ask your co-parent questions about them. If you position it as you want to know more about them since they are spending time with your kids, your co-parent may be less inclined to feel like you're telling them what to do. Plus, asking questions may provoke them to contemplate the answers.

Tread lightly here. The bottom line is that you cannot control the decisions your children's other parent makes so long as it doesn't put them at risk of physical injury.

Your Fear of Losing Your Place as Parent Makes You Reactive

One of the most threatening aspects of breaking up with someone whom you share children is the prospect that some other woman or man might someday claim parental rights—Mommy or Daddy rights—over your children. Even now, I can remember the anxiety I felt over the mere thought of another woman interacting with my child in a Mommy-like capacity.

It's absolutely true that some exes will play off of this fear and use it to manipulate the situation. They may tell their kids to start calling the new guy Daddy or the new woman Mom. I've never been comfortable with this. If this happens to you, rather than getting angry and saying nothing or telling the kids, "He's (she's) not your dad (mom)! I am!" I would suggest asking your co-parent if they could come up with an alternative distinction for the new person. Explain what the term represents to you. On the other hand, it is just a word. If it doesn't bother you, don't let me convince you that it should.

The truth is if you remain an active and positive force in your children's lives, you will not be replaced by anyone no matter what efforts are put forward. Your kids love you and that love transcends the breakup between you and their other parent.

TRUE STORY

A friend of mine learned of her co-parent's new love interest from their young child. Rather than getting upset at her former spouse over the fact he didn't tell her himself, she instead accepted that this was just who he was...someone that avoided confrontations. She accepted it and initiated a conversation with the new woman when she saw her at a soccer game shortly after learning about her.

My friend was kind to the new woman and once the co-parent and his new partner moved in together, this mom made an extra effort to include the new woman in communications surrounding the child. By doing this, she not only made the new partner feel included, but she also enlisted her help as an ally in their parenting efforts. What a win-win!

COLLABORATIVE APPROACH

When learning that your co-parent has become seriously involved with someone else...

- **DO** remain calm and if this is impossible, remove yourself from the situation until later.
- **DO** give the new person a chance regardless of how you were told about them. Your ex picked you, after all, and you're not so bad. Maybe this new person is a good soul who is just looking to be happy like the rest of us.
- **DON'T** talk badly of the new love interest to others, particularly the kids.
- **DO** view this new person as a potential ally in the effort to raise your children.
- **DO** be respectful, considerate, and friendly to the new someone if you expect this from them.
- **DON'T** fear losing your children if you are doing your best to be a good parent.
- **DO** consider wishing your co-parent well on their new journey. It helps to solidify for them and for you that while you two didn't make it as a romantic couple, you intend to make it as good co-parents.

- **DON'T** let your kids get away with bad-mouthing the new person. That doesn't mean dismiss their concerns. Let them know that if they are concerned about how things are going with this new person, they should first take it up with the other parent. If that isn't something they can do for whatever reason or it doesn't resolve the concerns, invite them to discuss with you what they are unhappy with, listen attentively, and emphasize that you will always be there for them. However, firmly state that you will not tolerate gossip or mean behavior just because they are uncomfortable with the change.

- **DON'T** simply accept the kids' version of the story or side with them without checking in with their other parent. If genuine concerns for your child's physical, mental, or emotional well-being arise over this new someone, thoughtfully bring it up to your ex in a non-accusative way. The kids may be using tales about the other person to win favor with you, or they may be misinterpreting events or things said to them.

- **DO** fake it until you make it. You can't change it. Even if you don't feel happy for your co-parent, you might as well make the best of it and **DO** all of the above anyway. Won't things be better for you if your former partner is in a stable relationship?

THE CO-PARENTING CODE

If you have a chance to prepare for this conversation, think about how you would want this to go if the shoe were on the other foot.

- Would you want your co-parent to root for your happiness?
- Would you want their support? Would you want their help in figuring out how to share this news with the kids?
- Would you want this to not derail your co-parenting efforts?
- Would you hope your co-parent would like your new partner or at least be kind to them so that you can both avoid more negative experiences?
- Would you want your kids to give this person a chance and get to know them? Would you want them to respect them?
- Do you welcome another person's help in bearing the burden of raising your kids? This last one is hard for many. Maybe your knee-jerk response is, "Hell no! They're my kids and I don't want anyone else telling me how to parent them or taking my place." But just remember, there is no perfect parent. I know I'm not and I'd bet you'd admit you screw it up now and then also. So instead of looking at this new someone as a threat, consider the possibility that they may be helpful to your co-parent and even you on your parenting journey.
- Do you want your kids to see their other parent happy?
- Do you want your kids to enjoy a new positive relationship with this person?
- Do you want your kids to live in a home where love is demonstrated and where emotions are stable?

9

HEY HONEY, WANT TO MEET MY KIDS?

* * *

How long should you date someone before he or she meets your children? How do you explain this new "someone" to your child? What if your child doesn't like the new person? What if the new person doesn't like your child? OK, actually, that last one is easy: Dump them like a hot potato! What if your child just needs to give the new person a chance? What if your *child* loves the new person but *you* stop liking them?

After considering the many ways this could go badly, maybe it isn't such a great idea.

Of course, you are kind of already in this thing with this guy and you really like him. You see a future with him. Besides, you already broke the news to your co-parent. Don't wimp out now. Put on a brave face, and let's figure this thing out.

And don't forget, you're not the only one who may have concerns: If your new love interest is not a parent, the idea of meeting your children may be terrifying. Or, they may have a naturally nurturing instinct and look forward with great anticipation to meeting your offspring.

In any case, before you proceed, shall we review some combative choices to avoid? Follow me.

COMBATIVE APPROACH

Introduce Everyone You Date to the Kids

A constant parade of new adults into your child's life can be very confusing to a kid and spark needless anxieties concerning those who don't remain in their life for long. Besides, exposing your child to people you either just met or may not know that well could be dangerous.

On top of that, if your child is in school or older, do you want them thinking that you get around? Would you want them to share with their other parent how many people you've dated?

I suggest you set up some type of parameter for yourself. Maybe it's a minimum amount of time or number of dates you've had with a new person. Just make sure to set a parameter that keeps the introductions of new partners to a minimum and to those who you want to keep around for a while.

Having a New Love Interest Meet Your Kids Too Soon

In addition to the safety concern I already mentioned, introducing a partner to your kids too soon can create expectations you all may not be ready for. It's like taking your new girlfriend or boyfriend home to Mom. You don't do it until you've 1) determined that you like them enough to bother, 2) decided that they are neither a loser nor an asshole, and 3) you're pretty sure you want to keep them around for a while.

Forcing Your New Someone to Meet Your Kids Before They Are Ready

I'm sure some parents want to get to this as a test to determine the viability of their relationship. But putting a person in this position before they are ready could be viewed as pushy or even manipulative. Get on the same page.

Introduce the New Someone to the Kids as Their New Daddy or Mommy

This one is a sure setup for trouble. If your co-parent is still alive and a reasonably good parent, your kids will naturally want to defend them. As such, they may become very judgmental toward this new person. They might also view this as hurtful to the other parent, which could damage your relationship with your kids.

Honestly, even if the other parent is no longer in the picture for whatever reason, I wouldn't recommend introducing your new boyfriend or girlfriend to your kids this way. It's too much pressure on everyone involved. Just introduce them and let them get to know each other. They can define for themselves what their relationship will be without you forcing it on either of them.

Failing to Plan—Accidental Introductions

I know it can happen. But do your best to avoid accidental introductions, like having the new guy sitting on the couch in the living room when the kids come home from school. All they see is that there is a stranger in their house. Choose better.

Also, if you're not ready to introduce the new person as a love interest, having them at your house a lot or meeting you at every soccer game your daughter plays is sure to raise your kid's curiosity. If it's too soon to introduce them, be more discrete.

Introducing Them in Public or in Front of Others

Just as sharing this news in public with your co-parent isn't a good idea, don't put your kids on the spot in this way either. It doesn't give them the courtesy of privacy in dealing with what could be to them an emotional experience.

95

Pretending Your New Love Interest Is Just a Friend

If your kids are toddler age or younger, this may not be a big deal. But if they are older than that, they could pick up on boyfriend-girlfriend dynamic more easily than you think. If you have led your kids to believe the relationship is strictly friendship, they could feel deceived once they are told or figure it out. Again, if you're not ready to tell your kids you have a new boyfriend or girlfriend, don't bring them around one another.

I know there are exceptions here. For instance, if you really do start as friends and your relationship grows into something more, I get this. But you'll probably still want to plan on some intentional way to tell your kids that your relationship is taking on a new significance.

TRUE STORY

I decided on a minimum six-month dating rule for myself before I would introduce anyone to my son. This, I felt, was safer and more considerate to him *and* the other person. There would be no constant parade of potential stepparents and no mixed signals sent to the other person. My child would see that I was being selective and careful. I also wouldn't be subjecting him to repeated disappointments. Above all else, though, I wanted to find out more about someone before putting my son at risk with a stranger to him.

In my first long-term relationship following the end of my marriage, I decided it was time for my son and the new guy to meet. He had a daughter whom I had already met. Since my son was only six and she nine, I didn't want to make this some big life-changing event—at least not in their young minds. I just wanted all of us to get together and have a nice time. I figured the kids might play and get to know each other and my son might at least become semi-comfortable with the presence of another man around me. To accomplish this, I planned a gathering of friends to play cards and

I didn't want to make this some big life-changing event—at least not in their young minds.

invited the boyfriend and his daughter to join us. I asked everyone to make it seem like nothing more than a bunch of friends getting together at Mom's house with a chance for my son to meet a new playmate.

Everyone arrived around seven or so, and we had a lovely time playing cards while the kids played. And played. And played. In fact, it seemed these two were long-lost relatives. They really were like immediate best friends. All my friends noticed and commented on how natural they seemed to be together and how much fun they were having—entirely oblivious to the existence of anyone else. Finally, the friends left, and it was just the four of us. The new guy and I watched a movie on the couch in the living room while the kids continued to play in the next room. The kids had the time of their lives playing with action figures together and giggling their heads off. The night was a success and a relief. Now we could all spend time together without fear that someone was going to hate someone else.

Looking back on this, I'm realizing that I didn't come right out and tell my son that I was seeing this new guy. We didn't hide it and I never said he was not a boyfriend. I just never specified that he was. So, while I discourage pretending someone isn't a boyfriend or girlfriend, you don't necessarily have to come right out and declare it in words either. They're likely to figure it out.

COLLABORATIVE APPROACH

- **DO** discuss parenting with your new love interest early in your relationship and before you introduce them to your kids. By doing this, you can gain insight on their expectations and desires. You may even learn enough to tell you if you two have a shot at a long-term relationship together which includes your kids.

- **DO** wait a reasonable amount of time to get to know the other person first. Only you can decide what is reasonable for your situation, but I'd suggest waiting six months as a rule-of-thumb before any introductions.

- **DO** tell your co-parent that you plan to introduce your new someone to the kids.

- **DON'T** introduce a new romantic partner to your kids unless the new partner agrees that they are ready. Talk about it.

- **DON'T** introduce the new person as your children's new Mommy or Daddy. It's too much pressure and assumes too much.

- **DON'T**, in most cases, bring the new guy or gal around your kids until you're ready to introduce them as your new love interest. Of course, if your relationship with this person legitimately started as a friendship that blossomed into something more and your kids have watched things evolve, they're probably already on to you. That's different.

- **DO** try to prepare both parties—your kids and your new partner—for the introduction ahead of time. You can tell your kids you have a special person you've been seeing that you want them to meet. You'll need to calibrate this language considering your child's age. Share a little about your child with your new partner. Tell them about their hobbies. Share a bit about their personality such as if they are shy or outgoing. I would also encourage you to be up front with any special physical or mental circumstances your child faces and how you address those.

- **DO** plan an activity you can all do together that both the kids and your new partner will enjoy. This will set the stage for keeping things light and fun. This could be playing a board game, going bowling, attending a sporting event, or doing some other fun group activity. Make it something that will give everyone an opportunity to talk and get to know each other a bit. For this reason, I would not suggest watching or going to a movie or show as your first meeting.

- **DO** introduce all kids, if possible, at the same time to the new person so that no one feels they missed out on an important family moment.

- **DO** plan for the initial meeting to take place privately, even if it's just a brief time before or after a more public activity. If your plan is to meet up with your new partner wherever you've told your children you are going together, **DON'T** drop the news on your kids in the middle of the activity when your new partner suddenly shows up.

- **DO** maintain a realistic expectation of the first meeting. Your kids and your new partner may both be anxious about it. If they don't click immediately, this doesn't mean you're doomed. Consider that they may just need to get to know each other better or get past the initial jitters of meeting a new person.

- **DO** anticipate that your children could be upset by the idea of a new person entering the scene. Reassure them that you are not replacing their other parent and that you care about what they think. Invite them to share their feelings.

- **DO** observe your children's interactions with the new person during those early days when they are getting to know each other. Ask them what they think of him or her. But be careful not to defend your new love interest to your kids. This is sure to make them feel like you're not on their side. Listen thoughtfully and tell them how much you appreciate them sharing with you how they feel.

- **DO** check in with your new partner on their feelings toward your children after they meet them. How did they feel about the interaction? Do they have any concerns? Addressing issues early will set the stage for open and honest communication and reduce the risk of there being misunderstandings.

- **DO** promptly address with your new companion and your child a situation in which any real disdain develops between them, or if the new person imposes their parenting style on your child too quickly or too much. This could strongly signal future trouble for all of you. You'll have to decide if a conversation with everyone together or separate conversations serves the particular situation better.

- And one last word of caution: **DON'T** be too quick to leave your kids alone with the new guy or gal. Listen, we've all heard the stories or know someone who was mistreated by a parent's boyfriend or girlfriend while they weren't looking. Stay vigilant.

THE CO-PARENTING CODE

● ● ●

Some of you may be children of divorce or a breakup. It will be easy for you to put yourself in the shoes of your kids. For those whose parents stayed together, you will have to do a little more work to view this from your child's point of view.

- Consider the ages of your children and adjust accordingly. Younger children may only need to be told that the new person is a special friend. But you'll need to elaborate on this in later conversations if things progress to an engagement or change in living arrangements. Older kids can process the idea of a boyfriend or girlfriend. So be up front with them to show you respect their maturity.

- Consider the emotional state of your children. If one hates change, they will probably not view this as a positive development no matter how awesome the new guy or girl is. It may take them longer than your adventurous offspring.

- If you're on friendly terms with your co-parent, you may ask them if the kids have mentioned anything about the new person to them. This may give you more information to understand how they're processing the change. It's perfectly valid for the two of you to discuss how your kids are dealing with this new development as long as the other parent is comfortable talking to you about it.

Notes

10

CO-PARENTING AND THE HOLIDAYS

*   *   *

Holidays—a time for joy, fun, and celebration—are a challenging time of year for any family. Everyone talks grandly about family, particularly during the holidays: beautiful holiday dinners, hours spent decorating together, shopping for gifts, and laughing jubilantly as they play family games with extended family.

Yeah, we all know the truth. Many family traditions play out more like a scene from the movie *Christmas Vacation*, fraught with dysfunction of all types. Fights between relatives, catty exchanges among the women, and the men constantly working to one-up each other's manliness whether that's through material success or who can belch the loudest, if that is their talent.

For divorced people with children, the holidays serve up the added challenges of dividing time with the children among parents, grandparents, and other extended family members and facing the devastation of missing out on precious memories with your child. As parents, isn't it our duty to create family traditions? Yet that is difficult to do when you've agreed to alternate holidays. At best, your tradition is either only executed in alternating years, or you carry it out on a different day from year to year. While this may work fine for you and your child or children, it is hard to pull off when considering the broader family. Grandma and Grandpa may always host Thanksgiving at their house five hundred miles away. A particular holiday tradition may only take place on Christmas Eve each year. We all hope to establish lasting traditions with our children that we can enjoy together for decades and that they can take forward with them throughout their lives.

It gets exponentially more complicated when there are multiple divorces, remarriages, stepchildren, and even pets that have to be worked into the equation.

The holidays are simply a minefield of anxiety for parents who live separately. How do you get it right? How do you build traditions when you constantly have to consider the forces outside of your home? How do you balance what your child wants with what you want to experience as a parent?

The holidays are simply a minefield of anxiety for parents who live separately.

I know I didn't want to miss all the significant memories in my son's life. My dreams of building that vast photo album of costumes and pictures with Santa didn't end with my divorce.

What will your holidays look like now that you and the other parent are no longer together?

COMBATIVE APPROACH

You could just assume it will all work out and that no added effort beyond keeping your parenting schedule will be required. You could also not worry about what your child gets in terms of gifts from anyone other than you. You could expect your ex to think about all of these things too or you could assume they'll do nothing. Among the many ways parents fall short when planning their children's holiday experiences after they split are the following.

Failing to Coordinate Holiday Schedules

Look, when you were with the other parent under the same roof, you had to consider their schedule when planning activities with the kids. Now that you live separately, it's even more important. Otherwise, your kids may be double-booked for family gatherings or holiday parties.

Even if you have a standing schedule with the other parent, those surrounding you who plan all manner of holiday events don't have this at top of mind when making their plans. So don't be so rigid with your custody schedule that you can't make room for unexpected yet very special holiday parties and activities.

Clinging Steadfastly to Traditions

Why is this combative? Because doing so may be unrealistic and put undue hardship on those around you to accommodate circumstances which no longer make sense. It also fails to consider the needs and desires of everyone else in this scenario, including your kids and the other parent.

Time and circumstances do not stand still. If you get too caught up in recreating the holidays you enjoyed as a kid, you're setting yourself up for disappointment. Not only has the world changed, but if you didn't grow up as the child of co-parents, your reference point is invalid. While you may be able to keep some traditions, you may have to carry them out a bit differently or concede them entirely if they no longer work in your current circumstances.

Additionally, as you cling to this outdated and out-of-reach version of the holidays, you miss the opportunity to create a new, improved, and realistic version.

Lastly, are you over-romanticizing your past? If you think about the last Christmas or Hanukkah you shared with your former partner and the kids, was it really magical? Or was it full of animosity, relationship stress, or hurtful behaviors going on under the surface?

Failing to Include the In-Laws in Holiday Planning

While it would be nice if your co-parent would take care of this, some will not. You probably have a good idea based on their behavior when you were together whether you can rely on them to let Grandma and Grandpa know what Junior wants for Christmas. Might your co-parent entirely forget to remind their sister who hosts the big family gathering to consider your kids' schedule?

You can stick with the idea that it's the ex's responsibility to handle this stuff now if you want. But in the end, if your kids miss out on a super-fun gift exchange with their cousins where Santa showed up in person, the first thing they are going to think isn't going to be that Dad failed to plan. They will just remember that they were at Mom's. Once again, Mom and Dad's divorce has ruined their lives.

Furthermore, they could think they were forgotten or intentionally left out of the celebration. Wouldn't it just be better to proactively communicate with the in-laws to coordinate schedules, gift exchanges, and the like?

Failing to Include *Your* Extended Family in Your Holiday Planning

Sure, we covered the pitfalls of forgetting the in-laws. But what about your parents, siblings, and others with whom your children interact? Don't they deserve the same courtesy? Make sure they know your schedule with the kids and encourage them to consider it when planning holiday activities. Share gift lists and let them know when some things can't be worked out, kindly explaining to them why it is important that you keep your co-parenting commitments. This is especially helpful to those relatives who've never had to consider these circumstances.

Neglecting to Work with Your Co-parent to Coordinate Gift Giving

Actually, the older your children are, the more this one applies. Often, the gifts kids ask for as they get older are more expensive—electronics, phones, concert tickets, etc. Some of these items may be out of reach for one parent without help from the other. If you really want your child to have something and think their other parent will agree, why not ask them to go in on it. And be sure to reciprocate if you are asked and have the means to do it.

However, be careful to not put your co-parent in an awkward position by always out-gifting them. If you plan to buy your child an expensive gift which is beyond their financial reach, first don't make the other parent feel guilty for being unable to go half with you. That doesn't mean you can't give the gift yourself to the child. But at least share with them that you are planning to do it. If you're comfortable taking it a step further, and you confirm with them that they are in favor of the gift otherwise, you could still put the other parent's name on it with yours even if they didn't financially contribute to it. What's the real downside to doing that? I think in Asian cultures they refer to this as allowing the other party to "save face." Extending this kindness could go a long way in strengthening the bridge between you two.

Beyond coordinating financially, I found it helpful to also coordinate *what* we were each getting for our son. By doing this, he didn't end up with duplicates, unless having the item at both houses made sense. Plus, the things he wanted most weren't missed by both of us.

Checking Out on the Holidays Entirely

If your divorce or separation was recent, you may be very distraught facing the holidays for the first time in this new normal. Maybe you've been divorced a while and sink into a depression at the onset of every holiday season, just wishing you could return to a simpler time.

For some of you, your former partner may have created most of the holiday cheer in your house and now you're in unknown territory, ill-equipped to act.

Oh, seriously. Do I need to take you adulting? Not only are you denying yourself the joy of the holidays, but you're also being selfish by denying your children the wonderful experiences you can all share together creating new holiday memories.

If you've never been in charge of family planning, hop on the internet and start doing some searches. Talk to other co-parents to tap into their experience. Ask your child's other parent for suggestions if you're on good terms. After all, they should want the kids to enjoy all of their holiday experiences, not just the ones at their house.

If you have to spend certain holidays alone because it's your ex-partner's turn to have the kids, find some useful employment of your own. Spend it with your family or friends. Volunteer at a soup kitchen or homeless shelter. Deliver toys and food to families in need. Host a gathering for others in your situation or attend adult gatherings you never had the freedom to consider before. Attend church or synagogue or mosque. One year, when my son was with his dad on Christmas Eve, I went alone to see a chick-flick I had been looking forward to. It was glorious!

Turning Your Attentions to Your New Life at the Exclusion of Your Children

Some parents become too happy with their newfound freedoms when the kids aren't around and become consumed by the side of their lives spent without them. With your kids away, it's fine to partake in adult gatherings and other activities you can't do when they are around. But if you start getting babysitters for them so you can attend a full schedule of adult parties and don't also nurture your child's holiday experiences, this is a mistake. They will resent the fact that they have no fond memories to look back on or may simply fail to learn how to enjoy the season. You will probably face regrets and may even become ashamed as other parents share snapshots of their wonderful family holiday activities.

Forgetting to Teach Your Child the Joy of Giving

While you may not want to give your co-parent a gift after you split up, you should provide for your child to give them something. Set a budget between you if you want. Take the child shopping. If money is tight, help them make something to give. Failing to do this is a missed lesson for your child. When you give a gift to another person, don't you enjoy watching them open it and seeing their face light up? Don't deny your child the right to do this for their other parent.

Putting it All on the Kids to Decide

Sounds nice on the surface—let the kids do what makes them happy. Isn't that what we all want—for our kids to be happy? But it can sure make life difficult for everyone else trying to navigate complex schedules, traditions, logistics, and such when the kids can decide whatever they want whenever they want.

TRUE STORY

A couple I know lived this experience and the stepmom shared it with me. She would wait patiently to find out if her stepdaughter would be joining a holiday meal. After getting the word that she would be with them, the stepmom would plan the menu around the daughter's food preferences only to have the child decide at the last minute to stay at Mom's for the meal. This happened on numerous holidays. The dad's response would always be that the child *decided* that she wanted to spend it at her mom's and really, that was all that was important to the father—that his daughter enjoy her holiday.

It's not necessarily wrong that the daughter wanted to spend the holiday with her mom. But allowing her to change the plan at the last minute without considering others just reinforced to her that *she* was the only one who mattered. Her last-minute change of plans was very hurtful and disappointing to both her father and stepmom. But it wasn't the daughter's fault. She had been told every year to do what made her happy without being given other considerations to take into account. And honestly, was this her place? Was it totally her call? Why should figuring all that out be her responsibility? Why should she have to choose who to spend time with?

Another couple I know has taken a far more collaborative approach when it comes to the holidays. The two who divorced ten years ago when their children were young continue to celebrate holidays together with their kids, even after remarrying. They don't necessarily wake up in the same house, but they do rotate gathering in one home or the other where the kids open gifts from both parents and enjoy one big holiday meal together. I think this is fabulous.

For us in the first year of our divorce, our son was still young and into the whole Santa experience. And as we all know, these moments are fleeting. Boy, I really didn't want the first holiday memories our child had of life post-Mr. and Mrs. Harlow to be of sadness. Nor did I want to bear the guilt of denying his father the experience of waking up where his son was on Christmas morning to find what Santa had left.

So that first Christmas after our separation, I offered to let my son's dad stay in a guest room at my new house. It worked out great. Our son's Christmas was saved, and we both experienced the joy of seeing his face light up at the sight of a magical Christmas morning. The following year, we carried out the same scenario in reverse. I stayed on the couch at my son's dad's place on Christmas eve and then joined his entire family for a gift exchange and family meal.

COLLABORATIVE APPROACH

- **DO** remember that you are creating memories for your child first, and you second.
- **DON'T** cling ardently to family traditions and past versions of the holidays. Be flexible and allow your vision to evolve.
- **DO** expect to do more than your married friends have to do just to enjoy the same level of kid-parent experience.
- **DO** coordinate with the other parent on schedules, gift giving, and financing of large gifts if you can.
- **DON'T** forget extended family and in-laws in your plans or let them forget your child.
- **DON'T** allow your child to choose who to spend time with, when, and how much—at least not before they are into their teen years. And even then, provide them

guidance. Suggest arrangements that work so that everyone can spend time together and feel like they matter

- **DO** help your child buy or make a gift for the other parent.
- If you end up alone on the holidays, **DO** something that involves you giving your time and energy to someone else's needs. You'll feel a whole lot better for it.
- **DO** seek opportunities that allow your children to enjoy time with everyone during the holidays without feeling like they are being shuffled around continuously from place to place.
- **DO** consider celebrating together with your co-parent but **DON'T** force a joint family gathering if it is uncomfortable. This will only ruin things for everyone.
- **DON'T** check out on the holidays or leave all the kid stuff to one parent.

THE CO-PARENTING CODE

- Consider that making great holiday memories with your child is as important to your co-parent as it is to you. Ask them what they expect and share your desires with them.
- Remember that your child may feel pressure to spend time with everyone or may get as stressed as you about all the excessive planning. Be the adult and let them know you are working to make sure everything is covered. Remind them to enjoy themselves.

- The holidays offer many lessons. This doesn't cease to be true after your split with the other parent. Think about the lessons you want to bestow on your children and act accordingly. Teach them how to give and receive. Demonstrate the importance of family traditions balanced with flexibility and sensitivity to the needs and desires of others.
- Think about all the other people in your children's lives and what they might desire during the holidays with your kids. Do they want to take them shopping? Do they want to spend time with them? Would they like to buy a special gift?

Notes

11

HOW DO WE HANDLE BIRTHDAYS AND STUFF?

* * *

Besides holidays, there will be other special days through-out the year that you navigate differently as co-parents. In this chapter, we'll look at celebrating the child's birthday, parents' birthdays, Mother's Day, and Father's Day. Of course, depending on your beliefs and heritage, you may also celebrate certain religious and cultural days like Easter, Passover, and Independence Day.

While the details of each celebration vary, the obstacles you face and strategies for dealing with them are pretty much the same. I won't restate all of the considerations and suggestions given in the previous chapter because, well, that would be boring. Instead let's see what may be different about these particular special days.

To begin, the child's birthday, parents' birthdays, Mother's Day, and Father's Day honor a specific individual in the family. And with religious and cultural days, you and your co-parent may have had differing beliefs or simply not shared a particular ancestral tradition. When you separate you may not be inclined to carry on with that traditional Passover meal if you were only doing it for your former partner's benefit.

How do you make sure that both parents' desires along with what is best for the child are carried out with regard to these special days?

COMBATIVE APPROACH

The most common thing I've seen play out with co-parents that I find extremely sad is the blatant disregard some parents have for the other.

- **They don't invite the other parent to the child's birthday celebrations.**
- **They don't take their child to buy a card or gift for the other parent on their birthday or parent's day.**
- **They intentionally plan other activities for the child to be involved in to prevent them from spending time with the other parent on special days.**
- **They don't include the extended family in any celebrations.**

If your ex routinely exhibits these behaviors toward you, your first inclination may be to give it right back to them. You're justified in doing so now, right? But if you treat your co-parent in a way that you wouldn't want them to treat you, how is that contributing to your cause? You have to demonstrate the behaviors you expect. When you mimic bad behavior, all you're doing is condoning it and asking for more of the same.

Other combative behaviors include:

They Don't Offer to Share in the Expense and Planning of Kid Parties

Some refuse to help because they don't have joint custody or because they pay child support, which they think should cover the expense. Some parents don't do it because the other had always planned these things.

They Attend a Joint Celebration and Make It Uncomfortable for Everyone

Some parents will go and then pick a fight with the co-parent or make snide remarks. Seriously, if you can't go and contribute positively to the affair, don't go. You're not ready for this step.

If your co-parent attends your event and creates an uncomfortable situation, do your best to ignore it at the time and take it up with them in private later. Let them know that their behavior made others uncomfortable and that while you would like to

> *Seriously, if you can't go and contribute positively to the affair, don't go.*

include them, if it is going to make matters more difficult for everyone, then that will not be an option.

If it is too much to let it go for the duration of the party, pull them aside privately to let them know they are making others uncomfortable and ask for their help to improve the situation so that everyone can enjoy their time together.

TRUE STORY

Every year on the night before my son's birthday, I recall for him the events leading up to his birth. I tell him how I went for a walk at the mall to try to induce labor since he was running several days late. I share how I kicked until they gave me the epidural and then how his dad laid next to me all night throughout my labor. I highlight the drama of ten people running into the room alerted by a monitor indicating a drop in my son's heart rate, and I share how my mom sat across from us all night, staring at me with that worried look that only a mother can have. Then I end it with how they rushed me in for the C-section, wouldn't let me watch, and seemingly pulled a shirt out from underneath my gown (or at least that's what it felt like), only to find that the shirt was our beautiful and perfect baby boy.

When it came to celebrating our son's birthday, his father and I traded off on this responsibility just like any other. One year I planned and paid for the kid party, and the next year his dad took care of it. When the special birthdays came up, we joined forces. This would sometimes mean going in on a nice gift together that we agreed on. Sometimes it meant we would have a party at one of our houses and invite the other parent and their family to attend. We each welcomed the other and their family into our home as we would any other friends and enjoyed the moments together.

When it came to parent birthdays, we made sure our son honored the other by taking him to shop for a gift and by giving him the money to pay for it without hesitation. This may sound easy enough. But it's not as common as one might think among divorced couples. In fact, none of the other divorced people I knew either bought for the other parent or had gifts bought for them. I guess they just couldn't get past themselves. But for me, it was important for our son to have the opportunity to buy his dad a gift of his choosing and get to see the joy on his face when he opened it. I couldn't take that from either of them. It wasn't my place. If we had stayed married, I would have expected our child to want to give his father a gift. In divorce, this expectation was no different.

COLLABORATIVE APPROACH

- **DO** invite the other parent to the child's birthday celebrations.
- **DO** split expenses and responsibility for planning with the other parent if they are hosting a kid party.
- **DO** take your child to buy a card or gift for the other parent for their special day.
- **DO** make sure you provide for your child to spend time with the other parent on their special days. If a conflict can't be avoided, offer additional time for them to be together.
- **DO** be sure to include the extended family in any celebrations.
- **DON'T** be an ass if you attend joint celebrations. Even if the other parent or former in-laws provoke you, smile and remember what you're there for.
- **DON'T** match your co-parent's negative energy by following their lead if they fail to extend courtesies to you on your birthday or other occasions. Instead, demonstrate the behaviors you wish your co-parent would take with you.
- **DO** teach your child how to shop for or make and give their parent a thoughtful card and gift for their birthday.
- **DO** plan for your child to spend time with their other parent on special days like Father's Day.
- **DO** ask your co-parent in advance to pay half and/or to help with kid parties. Ask them if they would be "willing" or open to helping out. Then it doesn't sound like you're telling them what they ought to do.
- If your co-parent doesn't normally help with planning kid parties and they agree to take it on, **DO** start by asking

them to help with small tasks that you can still manage to pick up if they fail to come through. But be careful not to come across as condescending, like, "Do you think you can handle that?" No one likes that.

Instead, say something like, "I'll order the cake and buy decorations. Can you bring the ice cream and help me decorate before the party?" When asking them to contribute to paying for the party, you could say, "The cost for the food and decorations was $75. Can I get a check this week from you for $37 to cover half?

THE CO-PARENTING CODE

- Envision how you like your special days to go and help your child create that vision for their other parent.
- Remember that your child will want to do nice things for the other parent. Even if you don't like them, you will find it helpful to be more supportive if you remember that your child does.
- Demonstrate the behaviors you would like your co-parent to take with you and that you want your children to learn.

12

SUPPORTING YOUR CHILD'S TALENTS AND INTERESTS

. . .

Parents of most elementary-age kids want to give their child the opportunity to try lots of different things so they can figure out what they like and discover their talents. Of course, every time one of these activities is added, it's another situation divorced parents must face where they will inevitably be in the same place together lest they miss out on the whole experience that their child has.

What do you do? Do you figure out an alternating schedule? Do you just not go and disappoint your child by not being there? And don't forget, it's not just your former partner you'll have to face but probably other family members, and maybe a girlfriend or new spouse. Need this be another trip down Misery Lane?

Besides attending the events, there are the other things parents do to support and nurture their child's interests and talents. What part are you going to play? Will daughter Kayla look back and say, "Yep, Dad and Mom were both there for me. I owe it all to them"? Or will she think, "I don't remember Dad ever going to one of my musicals."

Will the other parent go these efforts alone? When band camp, lessons, or sports leagues come up, will Dad have to say no because Mom doesn't want to give *him* money to help cover it? And finally, for the families with multiple kids, will it be: "Mom said I can't be in soccer because it conflicts with Alex's baseball and Dad won't drive me because I'm with Mom during the week"?

COMBATIVE APPROACH

Not Going to an Event Because the Other Parent Will Be There

Yep, this will tell your child where they stand on your list of priorities.

Going to an Event and Airing Your Dirty Laundry with the Other Parents

"The ex's new girlfriend is a tramp." "My ex-wife is spending all the child support I pay her on a boob job." Yeah, everyone wants to hear that crap. OK, I know there are many people who enjoy juicy gossip. But there are those that don't. Now you've made them uncomfortable, and those that do like to gossip are sure to tell others. Next thing you know, it gets back to your co-parent or worse, to your child. Nice job!

Going to an Event but Acting Like You Don't Know Each Other

This is a milder but still rather passive-aggressive behavior. I get it that some couples simply can't put their anger with each other aside, even in public. Certainly, keeping your distance is preferable to a public scene. Although does that leave your child wondering if he can talk freely to each of you when the event is over? Does he have to orchestrate separate areas in which to meet up with you? Do the kids really need to wonder if the adults in their lives can behave themselves in

I get it that some couples simply can't put their anger with each other aside, even in public.

front of their friends? Trust me, when they are teens, you'll have plenty of other opportunities to embarrass them, should you choose.

Refusing to Help Pay for Extra Expenses

Most extracurricular activities and hobbies come with associated expenses such as lessons, camps, travel sports leagues, club fees, and pay-to-play fees.

Certainly, not everyone can afford all these things. But did you think to proactively discuss it?

Enrolling the Child in Every Activity Ever Invented

The flip side is the parent who loads up the children's schedules and loads themselves down with massive money outlays for travel sports leagues and such, and then gets mad when the other parent says they can't help even though they never told them they would need help before saying yes to the child.

Failing to Communicate About the Activities You Each Commit Your Child to

A father may have grave concerns about a son playing football before a certain age. Mom may have already told Samantha that she couldn't join the equestrian team when Dad signs her up, unaware of this denial.

Not Sharing Information with the Other Parent

Many parents will withhold or simply fail to offer their co-parent the information they receive about their child's activities. Failing to share such basic information as sports schedules, coach communications, and deadlines with your child's other parent makes it unnecessarily hard for them to support your child's efforts. How can you expect your other parent to demonstrate good parenting without having all of the information?

TRUE STORY

One couple I know did really well with some aspects of managing the extra stuff and struggled with others. The mom enrolled the son in expensive travel soccer leagues without consulting the dad. Then she claimed to be broke when the son needed special cleats in order to play. The dad had no problem with buying them and took care of the purchase. But he still resented not being asked about joining in advance. The cleats weren't the real problem though.

The bigger issue was the fact that the son was enrolled in a travel league which had games scheduled out of town every weekend. The father had remarried, and his new wife also had a son. They had recently purchased a lake house about an hour away where they had hoped to spend weekends bonding as a blended family. Because the two parents of the soccer son never discussed either the lake house plan or the travel team commitment, they had both failed to consider the whole picture. As a result, the son would now find himself in the middle of things, either missing out on the lake house family time or causing his family to miss out as they would instead be attending his games.

While both parents had good intentions, they also both failed to communicate with one another and to treat their son or each other as they would want to be treated. I'm sure they didn't want their actions to cause him to feel uncomfortable or sad.

Be sure that your co-parent plan includes plans for talking about and paying for extracurricular activities. Note important dates well in advance for the activities that your child is interested in, such as enrollment deadlines and game schedules, on your co-parenting calendar.

COLLABORATIVE APPROACH

- **DO** go to your children's practices, games, and performances and enjoy watching him or her do their thing.
- **DO** use these moments as opportunities to bond with your co-parent over something you still have in common—maybe the only thing once you've split. Consider this an advantage you can use to enhance your co-parenting relationship and the experience for everyone. You will actually enjoy it more as you share in your child's achievements and cringe together at their struggles.
- **DO** proactively discuss who can pay for what level of extracurricular activities. Discuss any limits you want to set on expenses as well as scheduling. Decide how transportation will be covered for all the children's activities.
- **DO** communicate on schedules and deadlines, such as spring sign-ups, tryouts, and camps.
- **DO** talk about it when your child struggles with a particular activity. Form a unified approach to address the situation, whether that be to provide opportunities for improvement, allow your child to bow out of a given activity, or console her if she fails. Two cool heads are better than one. Remember, you have common ground. You want your child to be happy.

- **DO** communicate game and performance schedules with the extended family. I know I say it in almost every chapter, but it is so important and does require extra effort. They will probably want to come at least some of the time and your child will most likely enjoy having a fan club to cheer them on...until they become teenagers. Then everything will make them cringe and you can all laugh together.
- **DO** consider doing something nice like sharing photos or videos of the event if a parent has to miss a special game or performance for reasons beyond their control. You could also tell your child that their other parent would be so proud of them and really wanted to be there. Isn't that what you'd like them to do for you?

THE CO-PARENTING CODE

- Consider what type of assistance your co-parent will need to support your child. Advance notice? Paying? Driving? Volunteering? Cheering? Consoling? Telling your child no?
- Who else in the family wants to support your child's special talents and interests? Keep them informed.
- Consider the decisions most parents want to be in on when it comes to their kids and make sure to get input from your co-parent on these matters.
- If you need help covering things, plan ahead and ask your co-parent for help. Don't assume they'll help or make them feel like they have to say yes.
- Be sensitive to those around you and avoid making them feel awkward due to your issues.

13

WHOSE DOG IS IT ANYWAY?

* * *

Whether you shared a family dog with your co-parent when you were together or you acquire a pet after you've split, it's worth realizing that the kids consider the family pet to be part of their family. For this reason, you have to be careful not to discount your child's love for the animal. If you do, you run the risk of your child feeling like what's important to them doesn't matter to you.

Granted, you may not have conflicts with your co-parent concerning pets, or they may be minor. Still, be mindful of disregarding this topic completely as silly. I actually encountered one of these situations when our son was little.

Here are a few areas where co-parenting may play a role where pets are concerned:

- Whether or not the pet is allowed at both houses.
- Whether the other parent is available for pet sitting?
- What options are available, if for whatever reason, the pet can no longer remain with one parent?
- What type and how many pets are appropriate for your child?

- If the pet becomes ill and one parent cannot care for it either financially or otherwise, is the other parent a willing contributor to help with what is needed?
- If there is a pet emergency, are you each going to offer scheduling flexibility so that the children can be with the pet?

COMBATIVE APPROACH

Parents may simply feel like they don't need to deal with this. Maybe they didn't choose the animal and would have never chosen that snake. And probably in the majority of cases, there's no expectation from the other parent that one owes the other anything. However, your child may feel differently... particularly in times of need.

Making Assumptions About Pet Matters

One thing that could set you up for trouble down the road is not talking with your child's other parent about pets. This is particularly problematic if you make a bunch of assumptions, like assuming they'll watch the pet when you're on vacation or they will be fine with allowing your child to bring their pet into their home.

I can tell you for certain, while I am extremely supportive of my son and I'm friends with his dad, I would never house, even temporarily, a snake or spider.

Those who keep their house in meticulous order may take exception to a slobbery boxer bursting through the door when your child arrives for the week.

Using Pets as Pawns

Yes, this happens. At the extreme end, I know of one mom who threatened that if the son spent too much time at his dad's, the mom would take the dog to the animal shelter. The child lived in fear for months wondering if he would come home and be told the dog was gone or even put down.

Milder but still combative behaviors rear their ugly head when a parent buys their child some overly expensive and/or very time-consuming animal expecting the child to provide care for the animal even when they aren't there. Was this a ploy to score points or steal time from the other parent? Maybe not. Maybe. Without a proactive discussion between the parents, one can only guess.

The best way you can defend against such behaviors from a co-parent is to have direct and proactive conversations with them about pets. If your child mentions they may be getting a pony, you probably should ask your co-parent to have a conversation and elaborate on the plan. Be honest if you have concerns and clarify what you will and will not support when it comes to the child and pet scenario. At least then, you've set expectations with the co-parent. They may disregard them. But you've done your part.

Failing to Communicate

Look, I'm not saying it's unacceptable to buy your daughter the pony she's always wanted if you have the means. But I would advise letting your co-parent know about your plan. Also, get it for the right reasons. This animal lives in your care. You should want to own it and commit to caring for it in your child's absence without help, unless the other parent has agreed to a different arrangement.

You can certainly ask if they want to be involved with the pet or can help on occasion. But you should not feel at liberty to commit your co-parent to anything just because you decided to give the son you share a tarantula.

> *You can certainly ask if they want to be involved with the pet or can help on occasion.*

Being Unsupportive of Your Child When Difficult Pet Situations Arise

Are you going to be that parent who says, "Not my pet. Not my problem."? Will you hold up your custody agreement when the kids ask to go to a pet in distress, telling them it will have to wait? Most people will not.

If your co-parent is this person, appeal to them as best you can on behalf of your kids. If your efforts fail, console your kids. Then try to make up for it when they are back with you. For instance, if a pet dies, hold a family memorial service for it.

Going further, if your child's pet needs medical treatment for a serious condition which your co-parent can't afford but you can, will you sit idly by? Is this type of thing your responsibility? I guess that depends on how you view your job as a parent.

TRUE STORY

When our son, Ian, turned seven, his dad gave him a dog for his birthday—a beautiful purebred female Doberman pinscher puppy. Ian thought this was the best present he could ever get. And frankly, I would have to agree.

Ian named the puppy Amber for her pretty red-brown color. However, Amber became a big dog who needed a lot of attention and exercise. Ian's dad, Bob, worked all day five days a week while Amber remained at home alone. As months passed and Amber grew, her powerful jaws found new and innovative ways to destroy Bob's belongings while he was gone. He tried moving her kennel to the basement in an attempt to minimize the destruction. But Amber found new and inventive ways to escape the cage and find things to destroy in the basement. Really, Amber was just lonely and acting out as a result. Bob faced a tough decision. What was he going to do with a dog that was destroying his house and was ultimately unhappy being alone all day?

One day, he told me he was going to see if his mom and stepdad would take her into their home. While this wasn't a horrible alternative, I felt it would still be viewed by Ian that Bob had gotten rid of his beloved pet and birthday present. He had given away his birthday present. We both knew he'd be heartbroken.

About this time, I started working at the house and was home every day. I had lost my sixteen-year-old Yorkie the year before and was without a pet to keep me company on Ian's weeks with his dad. I was also a female living alone and thought the idea of a Doberman living in my home was sure to deter any potential house thieves. Who needs a security system when there's a dog that looks like it will tear your face off staring down would-be intruders? (Never mind the fact that she was more likely to run and hide from them than rip their face off if they actually entered.)

So, I suggested that I try taking her. I had always been good at training dogs to behave and felt confident that with me being there, most of her bad behavior would go away. At last, we had found a solution to avert a seven-year-old's heartbreak. Amber would simply move to Ian's other home.

I brought Amber to my house, and she seemed to feel instantly at home. She stopped the destructive behavior and provided me with much-needed companionship. She got to see her boy almost every day since Bob would drop Ian off and pick him up from my house before and after work. I had a nice backyard for her to run in, and a friend who was a professional dog trainer set us up with a remote electronic fence to keep her safely in the yard.

For the next twelve years we made countless memories with Amber. I'm so glad she remained in our *modern family*.

COLLABORATIVE APPROACH

- **DO** let the other parent know if you plan to get your child a pet. As this is something you are getting for your shared offspring, listen open-mindedly to any apprehension they may have. Sure, it's your house and your decision. However, to nurture collaboration, hearing them out and acknowledging their concerns will certainly strengthen this relationship.

- **DO** talk to your co-parent if you would like to consider them an option for any kind of assistance with the animal.

- **DO** give the parent the right to refuse to be involved with a pet. You may disagree. But you would extend the courtesy of honoring this type of decision with your friends. Do the same for your child's other parent.

- **DO** recognize that your child considers their pets family whether they live with you or with your co-parent. Act accordingly.

- **DO** initiate a conversation with your co-parent to discuss expectations if the pet situation was not discussed beforehand.

THE CO-PARENTING CODE

- Have you discussed pets with your child's other parent? Have you set expectations with them in terms of what you are open to at your house?
- Remember that your child cherishes family pets as if they're family members. If you treat their pets badly, your child will take it personally.
- Think about what you want others to consider before bringing a pet to your home and be sure to extend those same considerations to your co-parent.

14

---/---

MUST VACATIONS BE A SCHEDULING NIGHTMARE?

. . .

Vacations are about a thousand percent harder to plan for a family when divorce is involved than when it is not. Why? Well let's see…first you have to consider your schedule, your children's schedules if they are involved in sports or other activities, and the other parent's schedule. Then, if either parent is remarried or in a serious relationship, you have to consider the other partner's schedule and desires. If they, too, are divorced with children, you have to work around the schedule of the other parent and the other children's schedules. Then finally, if the said vacation is a group event based on years of tradition with a broader set of people, you may not even be at much liberty to dictate changes to the vacation schedule. Holy cow! This family tree is a lot to keep straight!

Seriously, scheduling a family vacation is among the most challenging of acts to pull off when all of these dynamics are simultaneously in play. Never mind accounting for the location, the weather, and travel arrangements. What a fricking nightmare!

Still, family vacations are a hallmark of family life. They allow children and adults to reconnect.

Still, family vacations are a hallmark of family life. They allow children and adults to reconnect. They give us time to breathe, away from the hustle and bustle of work and sports schedules, email, and, if we choose, social media. Vacations allow us to focus more on one another. They furnish us with lifelong memories and photos to reflect on the happy times throughout our lives.

Planning family vacations after you separate from your children's other parent is not simple. And without advanced planning, compromise, and flexibility, you could end up missing the experience with your children and deny them this opportunity with their other parent.

COMBATIVE APPROACH

Co-parent vacation planning can be derailed by several factors. Namely:

Failing to Plan in Advance

I'm sorry, but you need to concede your spontaneity and get organized if you expect things to go smoothly in this department. There are simply too many variables to consider, some of which are now beyond your control or even influence.

Being Inflexible on Dates and Locations

If you always get your way on family vacations and your child never gets to accompany his other parent on your in-laws' traditional family vacation, are you being reasonable? If either of you are doing this year after year, not only are you failing to compromise and show consideration, but you are also manipulating the situation intentionally, and that's not cool.

Turning the Family Vacation into a Weapon

Some co-parents perpetually caught up in their anger toward each other simply seek to deny them any pleasures. If this is you, I'd ask you to think long and hard about whose joy you are denying and to what end?

Will your child derive any positives from you preventing them from vacationing with their other parent? Will your behavior make co-parenting with your child's other parent easier in the future? Do you think this will make them more or less inclined to afford you consideration when you seek it in the future?

If you find yourself repeatedly in this circumstance, you need to talk to your co-parent and work to lay out some expectations. Write them down if you have to. If you've been granted a certain amount of uninterrupted vacation time with your child each year in your custody agreement, remind your co-parent of this fact. This will alert them to the legally binding commitment they've made and the potential consequences. It will also reinforce the fact that you are only asking for what the courts agreed is good for your child.

Forgetting to Consider All Parties in Your Decision

In the "What's at stake" section at the beginning of this chapter, I listed many who you will want to consider in your vacation planning. It's just not good enough anymore to make your plans considering only your immediate family.

Letting Others Dictate Your Schedule

Don't use your failure to plan as an excuse for tapping out on compromise. Letting others who are unfamiliar with or not sensitive to your circumstances dictate your schedule is a copout. If this happens one year, it's understandable that it may not have occurred to you to enlighten others to your circumstances. But if you do it every year, you're just being inconsiderate to your co-parent.

Failing to Leave Time for Family Vacations in Your Child's Schedule

One parent packing the schedule such that it doesn't leave room for both parents to enjoy a family vacation with their children smacks of manipulation. At the very least, it's inconsiderate to both your child and your co-parent. Set expectations and honor them.

If your co-parent is doing this to you, you must take responsibility for addressing it. And you have every right to do so.

TRUE STORY

One father I know had years of difficulty planning family vacations with his children. His family had been vacationing in the same location during the same week every summer for decades. Before he divorced, his wife and he would take the kids on this annual vacation just as he had done as a child.

After they divorced, the father continued to look forward to this vacation with the kids every year. It was his opportunity to connect with them away from hectic sports schedules. It also gave him the chance to share with them all the joys he had experienced growing up vacationing in this spot.

Unfortunately, once the dad became involved in a new relationship, the kid's mom came up with reasons every year why one child or the other either wouldn't be available to go or would need to miss part of the vacation.

In some years, the daughter was enrolled in optional sports camps. In others, the son was. This went on year after year. On many occasions, the dad did his best to make it work and salvage at least part of the vacation. He or his new wife would spend entire days driving hundreds of miles midweek to either return or pick up the child who had the conflict. There were also years when activities the mom planned for one of the kids either caused the entire family to delay their departure or return home early. This went on for years.

By the time the daughter was a teen, she no longer expected to be able to spend the full week on vacation with her dad. Unfortunately, the daughter had come to view these vacations as less important.

In the above scenario, one could surmise that this mother was being manipulative. She set up circumstances year after year which denied the new blended family the best opportunity they had to connect and vacation together. We can only speculate on this mom's motivations. Was she fearful of letting the kids get too close to the stepmom? And if so, why? Was she trying to inflict pain on the dad? Is it possible she simply was not thinking? Maybe she never liked this vacation experience and assumed her kids didn't like it either.

What if for a minute we give Mom the benefit of the doubt? Let's review the dad's role in all of this. Did the dad proactively plan the vacation? Well, sort of. It seems that since his ex-wife had been on these vacations for the duration of their relationship, he assumed she would expect the kids to continue going after they were no longer together. He didn't specifically confirm it each year with her though. These parents also chose not to use a joint calendar to coordinate schedules —something that could have clearly communicated the expectation. While the mom does seem to have set out to impede the family vacations, the father could have done more to prevent this from happening or at the very least, from continuing to happen. Still, the mom should have known after the first year that her co-parent's new partner went that she would continue to go for as long as they were together. Yet mom never inquired before setting out to plan conflicting activities for one of the children.

Did the dad talk to the mom when the conflicts kept happening? Did he share with her how it made him feel to miss these moments with his kids or what he hoped these trips would offer his kids? Did he share with his co-parent that the first year this happened with the daughter, she cried and was heartbroken she would miss going to a spot she loved with people she loved?

No. By nature this kind father was not confrontational. And like many fathers, he feared that if he pushed for more parenting time, she may look for other ways to reduce the time he had with his kids. So rather than confronting his co-parent, he instead accommodated the craziness. He changed up the family's plans to make it work as best he could. Of course, this entailed inconveniencing his new immediate family and interrupting their plans. It also robbed time they all could have spent with extended family and friends with whom they vacationed. But at least his ex got what she wanted.

While I admire this father's flexibility and efforts to keep the peace, in effect, he made it the rest of his family's problem rather than taking responsibility to resolve the matter with his co-parent. And I would conclude he did this because he felt those relationships were unconditional while what he had with is his co-parent was not. Still, this shifted the burden of dealing with the issue to family 2.0.

Truly, both parents could have done better. Neither of them did a good job of considering the other, communicating expectations ahead of time, or coordinating their plans.

COLLABORATIVE APPROACH

Next time you're planning the family vacation, here are some suggestions that may help planning go more smoothly.

DO Plan Ahead

Discuss the plan, even if it's just the dates, as soon as you know them. That way, if there are conflicts to overcome, you can start resolving those issues now and head into your vacation relaxed as nature intended it.

DO Allow for Flexibility in Your Plans

Yeah, I know. This one is hard because when I suggest that you be flexible, it may require you bending over backwards to make everything work out. But don't assume your large group, co-parent, or new companion is inflexible on dates. Explain your circumstances rationally to decide on the best dates that will present the least conflicts for everyone.

DO Stick Up for Your Relationship with Your Child

It's important to understand that when I say be flexible, that doesn't mean you should always give in to the other parent and forgo your vacation desires. If your conflicts are impassible year after year, suggest you set specific weeks for each parent to vacation with the kids every year. If this doesn't work, alternate having one parent get their way one year and the other the next. If efforts to coordinate still continue to fail, ask your co-parent for suggestions that don't require you being the only one to compromise.

If this still doesn't work, you may have to remind your co-parent that, like them, you too want to spend a nice family vacation with your child. Assure them that you are committed to making sure he gets to do the same with their child.

When the other parent sees that you are trying to consider them too, it may help them to realize that you are seeking a workable solution for everyone. They may even offer up reasonable solutions. If not, then you're probably struggling with your co-parent on a number of fronts, which requires a deeper conversation to get on a path that is more harmonious.

DO Remember What You Really Want

Look, you don't want to get your way if this means your child will be left feeling awful about the situation. If your child or children are going to miss a monumental family event or once-in-a-lifetime experience by not joining a particular vacation with their other parent, you'll want to do everything in your power to ensure they are included. Later on, when the whole family is sitting around the Thanksgiving dinner table together reminiscing about that time in Paris, your child will be part of the family story.

You don't want to get your way if it means destroying future prospects of cooperation with your co-parent or others with whom you are still connected within their group. Preserve these relationships through compromise.

THE CO-PARENTING CODE

●　　●　　●

Use these tips to get in an empathetic mindset that will help bring order to this chaos.

- On advance planning, consider if you like it when people spring things on you and impact your schedule without even thinking about how it might affect your life. Extend the same courtesy to your co-parent that you expect and deserve.
- Ask yourself if you are thinking of others and the impact your decisions have on them. Does your child feel like they've been considered? If your child isn't happy, you're probably not going to be either.
- Have you expressed to your co-parent the importance of family vacations to you and your kids? If not, don't expect them to make accommodating your plans a priority.
- Are you providing the opportunity for your child and co-parent to enjoy a family vacation together on a regular basis?

15

DISCIPLINE:
A UNITED FRONT

• • •

Of all the parenting topics I cover, this one is central to why parents need to get this co-parenting thing right. Otherwise, you take the risk of your child becoming a casualty of their parents' choices. When we talk about discipline, it includes setting limits, teaching responsibility, rewarding good behavior, and penalizing bad choices.

One of the saddest things I've witnessed in observing other divorce situations is the inability of divorced couples to effectively discipline their children and teach them how to make good life choices. Mothers who buy their kids everything they ask for so that the children don't consider whether they may have more material rewards if they lived with Dad.

On and on it goes. The child isn't given any responsibilities and is never told "no." They are constantly showered with compliments on how great and beautiful they are and never denied anything. From a lack of household chores to never living without something simply because "Mom said so," the kids of divorced parents frequently run the show.

You may be thinking, "So what, if everyone's happy all the time?" Is it so bad to have only positive interactions with your child? Frankly, YES!

To begin, if *you* don't teach your children about things like washing the dishes and doing laundry, who do you think is going to do that? Or are you planning to supply your child with a household staff after they move out? Or maybe you're OK with them wallowing in filth later on because they never learn the value of basic home cleanliness and how it can affect their physical and mental health. Could you be unwittingly raising a future hoarder to be featured on the television series *Hoarders, Buried Alive*?

Maybe you, too, were raised without being expected to help around the house and think this is fine. After all, look at you. You turned out OK. But I bet if you think about it, you had more responsibilities than you are willing to admit, particularly since it may cause you to question your current course of action.

But this is about so much more than learning how to clean the house. What happens to a person who is never told *no*, denied anything, or held responsible? You got it! That child grows up to be a spoiled, self-serving narcissist, ill-equipped to deal with the real world where he or she will most certainly be told *no* by someone.

Someone will eventually hold them accountable for bad behavior. Maybe they'll fail a class, lose a job, or worse, go to jail. Maybe they run up huge debt because they've never been taught to place limits on their desires. Maybe they will be told at work they can't do something because it is detrimental to others with whom they work. Someday they may be turned down for a job they desperately wanted. And you have failed to prepare your child for disappointment. They will be devastated and have no idea how to respond appropriately and productively to failure, going without, or having to think of others first.

Of course, discipline is easier for parents who share core values. You don't have to agree on how you each will instill these values. But the central principles need to be at least in the same ballpark.

Remember when you first learned you were going to be a parent? Were you struck simultaneously with fear and excitement as you thought about the responsibility of raising another human? Did you pray that your human would turn out to be a loving, considerate, and responsible person who contributes to the greater good? I doubt you hoped for them to grow up to become a self-absorbed jerk. So you better take intentional action to make damn sure you don't raise one. Few things you can do as a parent will more greatly influence your child's future than teaching them self-discipline and responsibility. It's also excellent common ground upon which to build your collaborative co-parenting relationship.

> *Few things you can do as a parent will more greatly influence your child's future than teaching them self-discipline and responsibility.*

But how riddled is the road of parental discipline with potholes?

COMBATIVE APPROACH

Co-parents at war with one another may discover that discipline provides ample weaponry to use against their parenting foe.

Among combative approaches are parents who…

Refuse to Discipline

Many divorced parents become so fearful of the possibility that their children will reject them that they choose not to engage in any conversations that might jeopardize these relationships. Many parents with limited visitation can't fathom making even one precious moment with their children unhappy during the short hours they spend together.

Unfortunately, the child not subjected to penalties for bad behaviors doesn't come to appreciate the consequences of their actions. All they see is that life is easier at one home. They listen to tales from their friends of being grounded, yelled at, or maybe spanked. They may think, "These things don't happen to me. I must not do anything wrong." They may also think, "Mom (or Dad) doesn't even care."

Someday, our child may make dangerous choices, life-changing choices, hurt others as a result and not expect to answer for it. They will have the parent who refused to discipline to thank for not raising them right. And so will their victims.

Set No Limits

Kids think they love not having limits. After all, they get to do what they want for as long as they want. They can have what they want. And they can use their parents' fear of falling out of favor with them to keep it this way.

Then one day, they set no limits on themselves and make a bad decision which impacts their life. It could be as mundane as not managing their time well, overeating, or acquiring debt. Or it could be that they overindulge and hurt themselves or others. This all because they were never taught to place limits on themselves.

Suddenly it occurs to them that you never taught them this.

Tell a Child That Their Other Parent's Discipline Choices Are Mean, Invalid, or Dumb

Wonderful, you've completely undermined the other parent's authority. You can count on the child discounting any future discipline imposed, even if aimed at protecting them from harm. We can only hope they don't decide to ignore their other parent if they've warned them not to play in the street.

Then of course, word may get back to your co-parent by way of the children that you've bad-mouthed their efforts. I'm sure they'll be open to collaborating with you now.

If this happens to you, reach out to the other parent to see if you two can get on the same page. If this effort fails, simply explain to your child that there are different rules at each home and that they need to follow the rules for wherever they are. But be sure to stress that rules related to their safety and fundamental rights and wrongs apply everywhere. Give them examples to help them understand.

Tell the Other Parent *How* to Discipline Their Child

You should absolutely discuss disciplining your children with your co-parent. But there are right and wrong ways to do this. Even if you were the main disciplinarian when you two were together, you've relinquished the right to impose your will on them. And frankly, most people aren't very receptive when told they must do something by someone else, particularly someone from outside their home. Your child may live with them. But you do not.

Let's face it. You can share how you are disciplining. You can suggest to the other parent what has worked best for you. And you should certainly discuss any matters which you believe are detrimental to your child. But you can't insist they adopt your approach or even your rules.

Still, some parents have radically different views of what is acceptable when it comes to discipline. One might believe in corporal punishment while the other sees this as child abuse. Another parent may refuse to discipline a child even when it puts their future in jeopardy. For these cases, you may need to enlist the help of family or legal professionals who can work with all of you to find solutions.

Leave Discipline to the Other Parent and/or Teachers

In many homes, there is one primary disciplinarian—either the mom or the dad. One plays the good cop while the other is the bad cop. Some cohabitating parents grow to resent this as they don't like the idea of always being the heavy—the one who spoils everyone's fun.

Add to that an already fragile relationship like co-parenting, and the resentment one parent feels is often heightened. They may view the non-disciplinarian as negligent or downright manipulative. They probably won't view it as an effort to be collaborative or do what is best for the child.

Use Disciplinary Issues Against the Other Parent

Unfortunately, some divorced parents use disciplinary issues to build a case against the other parent. They do this to take legal action aimed at reducing parenting time, increasing child support, or simply as justification for denying parent-child interactions with an ex.

However, a word of caution…you may have heard horror stories from other divorced parents where this was their experience. But if your co-parent has no history of doing this, don't jump to any assumptions that they would. You could miss out on the opportunity to work together toward a common goal—a precious commodity among co-parents.

If you are the one seeking to build such a case, be mindful of your motivation. Is it to protect your child from harm? Or are you afraid they will choose the other parent over you and so you seek to secure favor with them? Have you even spoken with the other parent to determine if your concerns are valid?

TRUE STORY

There was a time during our son Ian's middle school years where he and I had difficulty communicating. I think he was sure he was being judged by everyone, including me, all the time. Like any other preteen, Ian lacked confidence in these years and at the same time felt compelled to wield control over something, anything, even if that was a heated conversation with Mom.

After arguing with him for several hours on this particular day about helping out around the house, and him doing everything in his power to fight me on the point, I had had enough. We were getting nowhere. I don't really remember the details of our actual argument. But I do remember feeling like we had devolved into a circular conversation that was simply not going to resolve without a radical change in strategy. So I called in reinforcements. I asked his dad if he would talk to our son.

Bob didn't hesitate and came over to my house immediately. He laid it on the line with Ian and told him he was not to talk to me ever again in that tone or manner. He reinforced my points, telling Ian that Mom was right and that he needed to do what I said. In short, Bob was being a good father. It probably helped that he agreed with what I was asking Ian to do. But I think even if it wasn't something he made Ian do, he would have backed me up—assuming it wasn't something he adamantly disagreed with.

I couldn't tell you why what he said was so much more effective than what I had already tried. Maybe it was the fact that with the other parent now involved, Ian realized he was outnumbered. Once he saw that his dad and I were unified, he knew he was not going to win this one. He conceded, and life returned to normal for everyone.

COLLABORATIVE APPROACH

- **DO** discuss discipline and disciplinary problems with your co-parent. You can certainly share with them the rules, limits, and responsibilities you've established, but **DON'T** try to tell them how to discipline or insist they adopt your rules.

- **DO**, as much as possible, present a unified disciplinary front to your children.

- **DO** bring in the other parent for reinforcement when needed—assuming they are willing. When you're still married, you can call the other parent in for reinforcement. What about when you're no longer together? Can you still do that? You can and should! There's no better way to signify to a child that it's time to give up their fight than to outnumber them.

- **DO** agree to disagree on reasonable disciplinary differences These differences don't have to undercut either of you when explained logically to your children. Simply tell them that the rules are different at each home because the circumstances are different. Emphasize that while the rules may vary, you both support the other's right to choose what is best in each home.

  However, you should also state which rules apply regardless of where the child is. Your child needs to understand that in matters of safety, the law, and treating others with respect, the rules apply everywhere and at all times.

• **DO** seek professional help if you are concerned that the other parent is allowing unsafe or illegal behaviors or is abusing a child physically, mentally, or emotionally. This last one can be tough. I'm not saying that you need to seek outside help if the other parent makes your child feel bad. But if your child exhibits fear of being with them, becomes secretive about what happens at their other home, or begins to have other behavioral or physical problems, seek help!

• **DO**, if you can get there, support each other by helping to carry out penalties across homes. For example, if Mom imposes an earlier curfew than Dad and Mom grounds the child for a month, Dad could support this by continuing the grounding during the portion of the month the kids spend with him. Explain to the child that while you do have different rules, you've both agreed to support disciplinary actions taken by the other.

THE CO-PARENTING CODE

As you consider how you will form a united front when it comes to discipline, consider the following.

■ Do you share core values with your co-parent?

■ Do you want your co-parent to be an effective parent?

■ Do you want your child to be disciplined, responsible, and deterred by consequences for bad choices?

■ Does your co-parent want these things too?

■ Do your children deserve two parents who care enough about them to find a way to teach them these values?

Notes

16

PAYING TO RAISE CHILDREN

• • •

If you have kids together, whatever your co-parent and you achieve or do not achieve financially will impact your children's lives. So, if you thought your times of fighting about money were over, they probably aren't. And even if you don't fight about money, your co-parent's choices will affect your choices and vice versa whether you like it or not.

Time to think about how you will each contribute to your child's financial needs. We covered the home and education expenses in preceding chapters. So, we won't rehash those here.

Instead, we'll focus on how the choices you each make can affect each other financially. We'll look at ways to respond to some of these situations both good and bad.

COMBATIVE APPROACH

Here are some of the ways parents create financial conflicts with a co-parent:

Refusing to Pay or Underpaying Child Support

This is a real problem in the U.S. And while it is a legal and moral obligation to their kids, still many look at it as something they just want to get out of. They mistakenly view it as some kind of *benefit* they are paying a former companion.

As mentioned earlier, there are parents who don't use their child support for what it is intended: to pay for their children's needs. We'll deal with them in a minute. But first let's focus on the deadbeat dads and moms out there.

Refusal to pay can many times be remedied through court-ordered wage garnishments. But still there are parents who game the system to keep from doing this. They work jobs "under the table." They work for themselves and underreport earnings. They even refuse to work to avoid paying. I knew a guy who actually did this! Some go as far as to move, in hopes that the child support enforcement agency will lose track of them. Of course, if their income increases, they may go to great lengths to conceal this from their co-parent. If it is discovered, a co-parent can sue for additional child support—and so they should!

It's one thing to be down on your luck and finances. But refusing to pay and underpaying are illegal. You face financial penalties and even potential jail time. If you're in the military and don't keep up child support obligations, you are in violation of the military code of conduct

> *It's one thing to be down on your luck and finances. But refusing to pay and underpaying are illegal.*

and can actually be court-martialed for it. Think long and hard about the consequences that are really worthy of this fight. Also remember that the split was not your child's fault or choice. Why are you making them suffer the consequences?

Failing to be Reasonable with Child Support Payments When a Parent's Income Goes Down

Yes, a parent may be legally obligated to pay child support even in bad times. Unless the court has officially adjusted their obligation, a parent is still on the hook for whatever amount the court ordered they pay to support their children. But that doesn't prevent the other parent from being reasonable when unforeseen circumstances arise. Unfortunately, some co-parents have their attorney on speed dial to file a contempt order at the slightest breach in the parental agreement.

I get going this route when one parent has established a pattern of not paying. But if this is unusual for them, give them a chance. Show them empathy and provide whatever flexibility you can. Then if one day you find yourself in a pinch, maybe they'll consider helping you in return.

Failing to Contribute Financially When There Is No Child Support Provision

You and your co-parent may not have established a child support payment agreement when you separated. We chose to forgo a formal child support agreement as part of our divorce. We did this because we trusted each other where our finances were concerned. Instead, we agreed to coordinate financial concerns outside the courts. We would each track the expenses we paid for our child and reconcile every month or so. In our case we agreed to each pay half. I set up a spreadsheet on Google Drive that we could both access and update. This made it super simple to have a line of sight to what was being spent. Of course, this requires that you each trust the other to report spending honestly.

Either of us could have refused to pay our half and the other parent would have had to figure out what to do without any help from the courts. If you are unclear whether you can count on your co-parent to pay their share of expense, I'd suggest a more formal arrangement.

Whether or not you have a legal or less formal agreement to share your child's expenses, if one of you fails to keep up your end of the deal, it sows the seeds of resentment and anger. In the end, your child suffers as the other parent works to make up for the shortfall elsewhere. Further, it breaks down trust between the two of you. Then, when either needs help covering anything financially, the other may not be so willing, concerned that the funds may never come back to them.

If your co-parent is not contributing financially and you have no formal agreement, I would first suggest having a very direct conversation with them, explaining what their contributions mean in terms of providing for the child you share together. You should remind them of the agreement you have and why you had chosen to keep it informal in the first place. If this does nothing to motivate them and you really need their financial support, you may want to look into your legal options now. I understand it is harder to do after a divorce is final, and you will incur legal fees. But if the financial need is great enough, it may be worth it to you. Only you can decide. If you do go this route, I would let the co-parent know your intention to carry through on a threat of legal action. This alone may get them to pay up to avoid the hassle. It will take some courage on your part. But you have every right, and they should feel obligated to pay half of all child expenses.

Failing to Consider the Impact of Your Financial Choices on Your Kids and Co-parent

I know you'd like to think of yourself as completely free of your ex. The fact is you impact your co-parent in just about every aspect of life with the exception of romantically—at least until your child is completely on their own.

That's not to say you have no freedom to choose your career and design your life for the earnings you are comfortable with. But not considering your child's complete financial picture when doing so is unfair to them and your co-parent, who may have to pick up the slack.

To say it another way, if you have financial difficulties and are unable to pay for certain things, this burden is transferred to your co-parent whether they like it or not. If he has remarried or entered another significant relationship, a new spouse and children may also be impacted. And the dominoes continue falling as now the standard of living your child enjoys in their care is also impacted.

Would you appreciate them doing that to you without so much as a thought?

Assuming a Child Expense Will Be Shared

Some moms believe that manicures and pedicures for their daughter are necessary. Others view this as an extravagance. Parents will buy things for their kids or sign them up for things and then expect the other parent to pay half. Then if they don't, they get angry at them and talk them down to others or even the kids. This is both inconsiderate and unfair.

Did you ask them if they were willing and able to pay half? If not, maybe you should have only chosen these things if you could pay for them on your own.

Some parents will promise their kids things they can't afford on their own knowing that the other parent will feel obligated to pay to avoid disappointing their child. This is just manipulative. How would you like it if they set you up that way?

TRUE STORY

I knew a father once who did all kinds of things to avoid paying child support. He avoided becoming gainfully employed. He took jobs that paid him "under the table." He intentionally did not update his employment information with the Child and Family Services Agency that enforces child support payment. He certainly didn't inform them of salary increases. He even moved out of state at one point without providing a forwarding address to the mom.

Each time the mom discovered that this dad had received a pay increase, she sued him for more support. She pressed charges to hold him in contempt for failure to pay and had his wages garnished. I DO NOT fault her for taking any of these actions. In fact, I applaud her.

However, she was not all that great of a co-parenting specimen herself. The dad claimed he went to such great lengths to avoid paying child support because the mother continually refused his visitation, so he felt it was justified. She also from day one had never talked to him directly to remedy anything. She always sought a legal remedy.

I understand his frustration with the mom. She was certainly wrong to deny his visitation. But he was wrong for working to get out of paying his court-ordered child support. It's hard to say which came first in this scenario. Did she deny visitation because of his history of not paying, or did he stop paying because she withheld visitation? A classic chicken and egg scenario.

For God's sake! There's a child standing between the two of you. Do you not see her? Have you not noticed? Can you just look at her and figure this crap out? She seems to be paying the most!

COLLABORATIVE APPROACH

- **DO** pay your child support and keep your records with your local government enforcement agency up to date.

- **DO** discuss the full spectrum of financial support your child needs for their things and agree on how these things will be tracked, discussed, and paid for.

- **DON'T** assume your co-parent can and will pay half on things that are outside of the child support agreement. Speak to them before moving forward.

- **DON'T** tell your child they can have something you can only afford with help from your co-parent before getting their agreement to contribute.

- **DO** seek legal help if a parent fails to pay child support or keep their records current.

- **DO** seek legal help if a parent withholds visitation from you. But **DON'T** design your own remedy for this, such as withholding financial assistance.

- **DO** consult a family lawyer or divorce attorney when drawing up your child support agreement or seeking to have it revised.

- **DO** consider that child support may not pay for everything your child needs or wants. There will be additional expenses to cover.

- **DO** consider that choices which affect your finances indirectly affect your co-parent. They may have to contribute more to pick up the slack if your earnings decline. Conversely, if you become wildly wealthy, they may not be able to keep up with your standards. This may mean that you consider some other way to even out things at each home for your child, or it may simply mean explaining the different expectations they should have at each home.

- **DO** pay back any loan from your co-parent as soon as possible. Treat it as a top priority. This will build and reinforce trust between you.

THE CO-PARENTING CODE

● ● ●

As you consider all of the expenses involved in raising your child and how you two collaborate on these, consider the following.

- Are you providing enough financial support to cover extras?
- Are you being honest with your co-parent about your finances?
- Do you expect advance notice of expenses? Are you providing this to your co-parent?
- Do you accept that you each impact the other's finances through the decisions you make about your own circumstances?
- What type of standard of living do you want for your child?
- Have you agreed on which expenses will be shared?

17

CO-PARENTING TEENS

During the teen years, your child faces ever maturing issues, from their changing physical bodies and body image to their social status among friends and others with whom they associate. They begin to contemplate their futures in the adult world. They explore romantic interests. They begin to drive and sometimes experiment with various lifestyles and behaviors that put them at risk. They rebel; some distance themselves from their parents. They may struggle with self-esteem and they may be bullied.

It's hard enough to parent teenagers today without the added complications of doing it as co-parents.

Are you prepared to tackle these trying years? Will you join forces with your co-parent to multiply your efforts, or just hope for the best? Co-parents who don't have their child full-time may not see all that's going on. Because of this, it is particularly crucial that both parents make a concerted effort to collaborate during your child's teen years.

It's hard enough to parent teenagers today without the added complications of doing it as co-parents.

According to the CDC, in 2017 there were more than 6,200 suicide deaths among those in the 15-24 age bracket, making it the second-leading cause of death for this group. That's more than twice the number of people who died in the attacks on the U.S. on September 11, 2001. And every one of these kids had their whole life in front of them.

If that's not scary enough, results from the 2019 Youth Behavioral Risk Factor Surveillance System show that 18.8 percent of high school students seriously considered suicide and 8.9 percent actually attempted suicide.[3] Those stats are simply shocking!

The primary risk factors associated with suicide are rather long. It includes psychiatric disorders such as depression, substance abuse, loss of a close family member, physical and sexual abuse, lack of a support network, isolation, and bullying.

Do I have your attention? Do you see how important it is for both parents to provide the support your child needs and be vigilant with any warning signs. Now is not the time for the two of you to stop communicating.

There are other less life-threatening behaviors to deal with as well such as educational pursuits, eating properly, maintaining physical fitness, getting enough sleep, and managing social media use and interactions. Oh, and do you want me to offer the stats on teen pregnancies?

---

[3]America's Health Rankings analysis of CDC WONDER Online Database, Underlying Cause of Death, Multiple Cause of Death files, United Health Foundation, AmericasHealthRankings.org, accessed 2020.

COMBATIVE APPROACH

Parents Stop Communicating with Each Other During Teen Years

This is the worst time to reduce communication with your co-parent. In fact, one might argue that now more than ever, you need to increase communication with your child's other parent.

Failing to communicate often enough at this state can greatly hamper a parent's ability to notice warning signs of trouble—particularly when time is split across two homes. As parents living separately, you will have to increase your efforts to understand what is going on with your teens when they are at your co-parent's house. Engage your child's other parent in more, not fewer, conversations.

Parents Communicate Too Little with Teen Children

Some parents find themselves upset by their teen's loss of interest in them. Their teen cares more and more about their friends and social status and less and less about them. Rather than lean in to ensure communication between parent and child remains robust, the parent avoids conflict and stops making an effort to find out what's going on with their kids.

This happens to parents who live separately as well as those who are still together. As parents of teens, you will have to put in more effort to communicate with your child than you did when they were younger. It's just part of them growing up.

Don't take it personally that your child's interest in you has declined. This is not because you're not cool. It is because they are starting the natural process of separating from you. This process will continue over the next several years as they become more and more independent. And trust me, you want them to master their independence, even if it makes your heart ache in the process.

Fed-up Parent Tells the Child to Go Live with the Other Parent

Some parents just let their tempers run away with them and spout off such things as, "I'm done! Go live with your father (mother)!" They may or may not mean it. If you have a bad temper and find yourself about to go down such a path, take a deep breath before continuing. Have a conversation with your co-parent to let them know what is going on and discuss viable alternatives. Dumping the problem on the other parent unannounced is simply unacceptable.

If your co-parent does this, initiate a conversation with them. Find out what's going on. Was it a fit of anger or a serious decision? If they said it but really didn't mean it, avoid being too judgmental. We can all get caught up in the moment when emotions are intense. If they did mean it, you'll obviously want to have a more comprehensive discussion about what needs to change with regard to the parenting arrangement. It may indicate a need to engage the help of a family therapist.

Parents Who Stop Watching for Warning Signs and Fail to Get Their Child Help

Again, this happens to parents who remain together and to those who live separately. It's just that as parents who live separately, you are more prone to missing these warning signs or discounting them as you only see half their frequency.

If your child needs help, early intervention can be their best shot at saving them from a life of misery. Involving the other parent, school counselors, other family, and spiritual advisors—even friends who you've noted are a positive influence—can help to steer a child back to safe and productive behaviors. If the problems are severe enough, such as drug or alcohol addictions, professional help may be warranted. The sooner the better before such behaviors become engrained in everyday living and threaten your child's safety as well as the safety of others.

Parents Who Conceal or Deny Their Child's Problems

I know parents who have withheld their child's problems from another parent because they feared they would be blamed for the bad behavior. I understand this fear. However, when is it ever right for another parent not to know everything about their child? Plus, by not informing the other parent, you may be putting your child at increased risk.

I can only think of one circumstance where this makes sense and that is when telling the other parent threatens the child's safety. Unfortunately, there are parents in this scenario—co-parenting with a volatile person who tends toward violence or psychological abuse yet is still allowed time with the child alone. For parents in this situation, I fully understand doing everything to protect the child. Outside of this situation, you are not being fair to the other parent and I bet you wouldn't appreciate them hiding such information from you.

If your co-parent has withheld information from you, think about what you read in the first paragraph here. Is it possible the other parent fears you will blame them for whatever Joey has done? If this is what you typically do, then you can't blame your co-parent for not being forthcoming with you. You have not made it feel safe to do so. You have some work to do to gain their trust so that they willingly share important information with you.

Parents Who Don't Work Together to Support Their Child's Aspirations

As you come down the home stretch of high school toward college, you can be intentional or unintentional with helping your child plan for their future. If you are both unintentional, then don't expect your child to be intentional or get intentional results. Talk to them about what they want both professionally and personally. Share this information with the other parent. Maybe they have a friend or family member who can offer counsel on a career or school choice.

Overall, you can see that communication is the common thread across all of these. Don't assume that whatever arrangements you established years ago to handle co-parenting matters will be enough now. You should expect to communicate more, discipline more, pay more, and be more worried about your child than ever for the next five to ten years.

TRUE STORY

A couple I knew who had divorced had a daughter together. They had a shared parenting arrangement in which their daughter spent half her time with each parent week to week. As the daughter entered high school, Dad began dating someone new. The new woman spent a lot of time at Dad's house, and when the daughter was there, she felt like a third wheel, left to her own devices for entertainment.

When the daughter returned to Mom's she would complain to her mom about Dad's behavior and how she felt ignored when she was there. Mom asked her if she had talked to her dad, and the girl said she hadn't. So Mom suggested that her daughter try that first and if they couldn't work it out to let her know and they could all have a conversation together.

Still, the daughter didn't bring up her frustrations to Dad as he seemed to be much more interested in his new girlfriend than anything else.

The father began to notice that his daughter had stopped sharing much with him. She would come over and hibernate in her room for hours watching TV and looking at social media. He would ask her how her day at school went and she would give one-word responses. This was quite different than the relationship the daughter enjoyed with Mom. They talked about everything—who her friends were, how school was going, her world views, and what she wanted to pursue as a career. The daughter also expressed loneliness that she felt from being an only child. Because she was open with Mom, the mother knew what things to watch out for to make sure her daughter continued to thrive.

At some point, the dad reached out to the mom to express his concern with not being able to talk to his daughter and know what was going on in her life. The mom agreed it was a concern and suggested they have more regular conversations to fill in the gaps. As these parents had remained amicable, the dad was open to this idea and they began to meet up for coffee every couple of weeks to trade notes.

When the parents got together, Mom didn't throw judgments at the dad. She didn't focus on telling him the concerns the daughter had shared with her *about* him. Instead, she focused on giving the dad information he wasn't getting from his daughter directly—details she thought would help him support the daughter's well-being and her maturing into a young adult. Mom made sure Dad knew about the comments the girl had made about feeling lonely so that he could watch out for signs of depression. She suggested he consider finding ways to spend more time with the daughter—maybe even along with the new girlfriend. She shared with him the girl's career aspirations so that he could support her efforts to get good grades and secure college scholarships. And he learned quite a bit about their daughter's views of the world, which helped him to stay connected and understand what was important to her.

COLLABORATIVE APPROACH

- **DO** revisit whatever co-parenting plans you've laid out to determine if they are adequate or should be revised to address teen concerns. Discuss discipline including rules and limits imposed, physical health and habits, computer use, school, friends, finances, college, and how they spend their time.
- **DON'T** hold your child's distancing himself or herself from you against them. This is a natural part of human development as the child prepares to leave the nest.
- **DO** discuss it with the other parent before talking to your child if you believe a change in custody or parenting time should be explored.
- **DO** stay in touch with teachers, school counselors, and coaches to remain abreast of your child's behavior and to become aware of any warning signs.
- **DON'T** hide problems your child is having from the other parent. This inhibits their ability to assist in solving the problem.
- **DO** frequently ask your child how they are doing and share what you hear and observe with your co-parent.
- **DO** ask your co-parent what they are hearing and observing with your teen when they are with them.

- **DO** ask your child what their goals are. If they don't know, offer them help or suggestions on how to figure this out. If they tell you, share this information with your co-parent so that they can help too.
- **DO** remind your kids that you've been there too and understand some of what they're going through.
- **DON'T** live in denial. Explore concerns with both your co-parent and your child.

THE CO-PARENTING CODE

* * *

Here are some questions to ponder as you consider co-parenting your teen.

- Remember what it was like to be a teen? What was important to you? What upset you?
- Are you sharing your concerns and observations with your co-parent?
- Did either you or your co-parent have substance abuse problems or engage in risky behaviors as a teen? How did your parents handle it? Did they know? Was what they did effective? Be wary of hereditary predispositions such as alcoholism and depression.
- How did your parents support and interact with you as a teen? How did that work out for you?
- Does your teen have a support network that includes you, their co-parent, other adults they respect, and friends?
- Do you both know your teen's friends? Do any of them concern you? What are you doing about that?

Notes

18

---/---

WHEN SOMETHING BAD HAPPENS TO A CO-PARENT

• • •

Whether you have a good or bad relationship with your co-parent, when something bad happens to them or to you, it will impact not only the children but both parents. How parents react to their own misfortunes and those of a co-parent teaches a child how to respond to adversity and support those in need. It also reveals a great deal about the character of their parents.

Among the possibilities, parents could:

• Be injured
• Fall ill
• Get in legal trouble
• Lose a job
• Lose someone close to them
• Become mentally unstable
• Become addicted to alcohol or drugs
• Die

How will you respond in these circumstances?

COMBATIVE APPROACH

To make a bad situation worse, you could respond by:

Telling Your Kids that Their Other Parent Got What They Deserved

Really? Even if you think this, don't say it to your kids—at least not if you want them to learn anything about empathy and helping others in need.

Leaving Your Child to Deal with It on Their Own or with Their *Other* Family

You may be thinking, "Glad that's not my problem to deal with." Unfortunately, it is your child's problem and, by way of them, your problem as well. It's bound to affect you in some way even if only to figure out how to best support your child in the situation. Consider how isolated your child may feel if you're not there for them.

Telling Your Kid They Better Be Careful or They Could End Up the Same Way

If the tragedy resulted from bad choices, you may feel this is the perfect time to teach your children a lesson about consequences. It isn't! Using a situation so close to someone can be powerful. But you run a serious risk of scaring the crap out of them and planting a seed of inevitability. You can find other examples to use as teaching moments.

> *If the tragedy resulted from bad choices, you may feel this is the perfect time to teach your children a lesson about consequences.*

If your child is the one who brings it up, acknowledge their concern and offer them tools and insights to help them make choices that will lead them down a better path. Reinforce that they are an individual and not predestined to make the same choices.

Failing to Offer Any Support to Your Co-parent or Their Family

You might not be sure if your co-parent would be open to your offer or maybe you assume your co-parent had help from others. Sure, your former in-laws may be better equipped to provide the emotional support needed. They may not even want your help. But not offering sends a message that you don't care what others are dealing with and certainly does nothing to build or strengthen bridges across the family. Plus, it sets a bad example for your children.

If you don't get offers of help from your co-parent, you may find this hurtful or inconsiderate. I would suggest not assigning too much meaning to the omission. Just as you might've felt that way if the shoe were on the other foot, it could be that they were not sure if you would be open to their offer or assumed you had help from others. Try not to always think the worst of your former partner. Starting there keeps you entrenched in negative energy and unable to see other possibilities. If you need parenting help, ask them for it. They might have just been waiting for you to make the first move.

TRUE STORY

At 4 a.m. on April 18, 2016, two weeks before our son graduated from college, I received a text from his stepmom. My son's dad had been in a motorcycle accident the night before and was in intensive care. He was stable, and she would provide more information later after the doctors had been back in the morning. Because I knew her well and was familiar with her communication style, I could tell that while she didn't come right out and say it, there was an unstated level of concern with his condition. I responded right away with a message expressing my concern and asked her who had their young daughter in case she needed help. She sent our son the same text.

Of course, I did not go back to sleep. With such limited information, I could only ponder the endless possibilities of his condition. And what was my son thinking right now? Did he even get the text?

I set out on my short commute to work and checked in with Brandi to get more details on Bob's condition. She was calm and explained the various injuries Bob had sustained. They didn't sound all that bad on the phone. But she did say he was on a ventilator and hooked up to several machines.

I knew I needed to prepare Ian to see his dad in this condition; neither Brandi nor I had heard from him. Finally, as I hung up with Brandi, the phone rang. It was Ian. He explained that he had actually read the text at around 4 a.m., but since Brandi said Bob was stable, he didn't think it was a big deal and thought it would be OK to check in after he woke up.

KIDS! OMG! I get it. They think we're all going to live forever and nothing bad ever happens to us personally. Until it does!

I explained to Ian that he needed to respond to his stepmom right away and let her know that he got the message and then he needed to get to the hospital. It was odd trying to impress the urgency upon him without panicking him. I told him not to be shocked when he saw his dad and described precisely what he might look like. He was bruised up. His head was partially shaved with a gash in it. He wasn't breathing on his own. So there were tubes and wires attached to him to help him breathe, monitor his vital signs, and deliver medicine intravenously. Ian didn't say much. I asked him if he was OK, and he said he guessed so and that he was getting dressed to head that way. I told him to call me later if he wanted and then I let him get on with it.

I decided to give the immediate family time and waited until the next evening after work to visit. When I got there, Bob's family was all crowded into the room. I greeted everyone with a somber hello, although I was happy to see them in spite of the horrible circumstances which had brought us together.

When I got the prognosis on Bob's condition, I learned he would likely remain in the hospital for at least ten more days. I did a quick calculation in my head and realized that we were right up against our son's college graduation date. Wow! He might actually miss it. That would be awful.

Before the accident, Bob and Brandi had been planning an open house following Ian's graduation ceremony to celebrate. Of course, after the accident, all those plans went out the window. So instead, I offered to host a small gathering at my house. In keeping with Ian's wishes, I kept it to family members on all sides.

As the date got closer, Bob was able to come home, but just about everything was painful for him. Yet, on the day of Ian's graduation, Bob arrived in a wheelchair flanked by his wife and dad. He got to see his only son walk across the stage at Capital University to accept his college diploma.

As the day with family unfolded, I expressed to everyone how special it was that this eclectic family gathering could take place at my home. It really was a special day for a special graduate and his family.

COLLABORATIVE APPROACH

- **DON'T** make disparaging comments about the other parent when something bad happens to them or at any other time. If you wouldn't want to hear someone say a particular thing about you, don't say it about them.
- **DON'T** allow your child to say negative things about the other parent unchecked, or worse, agree with them. If you can't honestly disagree, silence would be better. Work to redirect their focus to being supportive of the other parent. Say something like, "I understand why you might feel that way. However, right now your mom (or dad) needs our support. Let's focus on how we can help them."
- **DON'T** make comparisons between your child and their other parent (that is, "Bad things could happen to you too!"). This is just too scary for anyone. Plus, they may already be thinking this and you're just increasing the emotional load. If they want to talk about this possibility, you can ask them what they think they can do to ensure this doesn't happen to them.
- **DO** offer your support to your child, your co-parent, and their family. In short, offer them what you would want from anyone else close to you in times of crisis.
- **DO** engage professional help for your child when life-changing events occur. In the cases of parental addictions, incarceration, life-altering physical or mental health problems, and deaths, your child may need professional help coping. Seek assistance from school counselors, spiritual advisors, support groups, social services agencies, and mental health professionals.

- **DO** consider whether the tragedy warrants either a temporary or permanent change in co-parenting arrangements.
- **DO** ask for help. If you are the parent who has encountered a difficult time and you need help, **DON'T** assume they should know what you need. People aren't mind readers.

THE CO-PARENTING CODE

When your family experiences a tragedy, how can you position yourself to be supportive and empathetic? Try these out for size:

- Ask yourself how you would want your co-parent to talk to your children if something bad happened to you?
- Think about how you would hope to be supported by your co-parent if you experienced a tragedy.
- Consider the fears and pain your child may be dealing with.
- What if anything needs to change about your co-parenting arrangement in light of these developments?

Notes

19

---/---

ADDING STEPPARENTS TO THE MIX

· ◦ ·

As if co-parenting weren't difficult enough all on its own, let's introduce a third party into the equation. Enter the stepparent.

The story of *Cinderella* pretty much sealed the fate for stepparents everywhere. They are all evil, I tell you. Mean to the core. They hate their stepchildren and want only the worst outcomes for them. OK, I'm calling B.S. before this gets completely out of hand!

The truth is most—not all—stepparents feel many of the same emotions for their stepchildren as primary parents do for their children. They feel their pain and their joy. They take pride in their accomplishments and worry about their futures. They want the best things in life for them. They just don't have a lot of say in the matter.

Many stepmoms and stepdads play as important a role in their stepchildren's lives as the primary parents do. I've been to more than one wedding where both the father and stepfather walked their daughter down the aisle. I know plenty of stepdads who coached their stepson's basketball teams, and stepmoms who made Halloween costumes for their stepchildren.

Having been both a parent and stepparent, I can say unequivocally that stepparenting is much harder and far more frustrating. You still feel all the burdens of parenting but wield next to no influence over the situation.

On the flipside, accepting a stepparent's presence and influence on the parenting of one's children can be very challenging—whether you are the ex-spouse or the remarried spouse.

Whether you have remarried, your co-parent has remarried, or you *are* the stepparent in the scenario, I'm sure you have envisioned how you'd *like* things to go. But be careful to have realistic expectations. In fact, be prepared to have some conflicts that you'll all need to work through.

COMBATIVE APPROACH

In my experience, I have witnessed some incredibly atrocious behaviors between primary parents and stepparents—everything from the unintended slights to the completely calculated lengths that some parents go to in order to prevent the stepparent and stepchild from developing productive and loving relationships. There are also tragic stories of the stepfather or stepmother who treats the stepchild horribly or seeks to cause mayhem with a former spouse. But I really believe these are the outliers rather than the norm.

Most stepparents really just want to have a happy family, be loved, and see their children *and* stepchildren thrive. Primary parents have the same goals, but many have difficulty figuring out how to accept the stepparent into *their* parenting equation.

What can the primary parents—both the ex-spouse and the remarried spouse—and stepparents do to make this whole new dance go well? What can they avoid doing? Let's start there.

Sabotaging Relationships Between Stepparents and Stepchildren

A former spouse may try to make a stepparent look bad by distorting things they've said. They may dig up dirt from their past to share with the children or former spouse. Some get downright snarky and criticize a stepparent's career, appearance, or social status. A scorned or fearful parent may do everything they can to make life a living hell for the stepparent in hopes that it will drive them away.

If you are a stepparent feeling sabotaged by the ex-spouse, this can be very frustrating. You already face the challenges of forging relationships with children midway into the game. And now you have someone working against you. Why? What new fresh hell is this? And how do you make it stop?

First, if you are a new stepparent, decide very quickly which problems need to be addressed and which just need time to subside. There is going to be an adjustment period for everyone. Think of it as the breaking in period for a new pair of shoes—uncomfortable at first, but eventually just what you thought they'd be. They need to gain confidence in your parental ability. Give them time and suspend judgment for a while.

If after a while you still feel the ex-spouse is working against you, invite them to a private conversation with you. When you meet, thank them for meeting with you and ask them directly what concerns they have about you. Have an open honest conversation being sure to let them know that you care about establishing positive relationships with both the kids and with them.

Disliking a Stepparent and Wanting Them Gone

If you are an ex-spouse feeling desperate to oust a stepparent from your family scenario, I have similar advice for you as I gave to the stepparent. First give it time. Second, if time doesn't cause your concerns to fade, ask for the stepparent to meet with you so that the two of you can talk it out. When you meet, be open-minded to what they have to say. Give your co-parent a heads up to let them know that you plan to do this.

You may also benefit from doing some self-reflection. Is your anxiety over the stepparent really about them or is it caused by feelings of envy, insecurity, or grief over the loss of your family? If so, you may need to do some mental exercises or talk to someone to help you release these feelings.

If you frame the stepparent as evil, you'll view every action they take and word they speak through this lens. And it may not even be warranted. Banish any thoughts you have of influencing your former partner's future with this person. That is wasted energy. Instead, recognize that you best serve your children by helping their stepparent to be the best influence possible on them.

If, after you've gotten to know this person, your worst fears come true—they really are a bad person—you and your kids will benefit the most if you stay close to the situation. Remain active in your children's lives, being present as much as possible. Maximize your opportunities to influence and shield them from harm.

If matters escalate to levels that you believe endanger your children's physical, mental, or emotional well-being, seek legal or other professional help.

Mistreating Stepchildren

Having your ex tell you he thinks your new husband is mistreating your kids can either make you angry at the ex because you believe the allegation to be false or it can cause you to wonder if you unwittingly exposed your children to harm. Before snapping to judgment either way, pause for a minute. Ask yourself if your co-parent has provided proof? Have you observed anything that supports this claim? Have the kids alerted you to any concerns? Is it possible that your ex is just trying to stir up trouble?

If the ex has provided proof or if a child corroborates what they have told you, address it immediately. But be sure to confront the behavior with your new spouse in a matter-of-fact way. You may find out it was all just some big misunderstanding. If this ends up being the case, set the record straight with everyone—the kids and the ex—and reassure your new spouse that you support them and want them to have a good relationship with your kids and even with your ex to the extent possible.

Of course, if you find out the mistreatment is true, you'll need to clarify acceptable stepparent-child interactions with them, determine if any amends are warranted, and reach agreement on how things must be going forward.

Disciplining Stepchildren

There are lots of parenting styles—some instilled in us by our own parents, some we developed on our own, and others we may have picked up from former partners. By the time many of us end up in blended family scenarios, we're pretty set in our ways.

Then one day, you join up with another partner to create that perfect blended *Brady Bunch* family. Suddenly, stark differences in parenting style begin to emerge. These differences may be so vast between you and a new mate that you wonder if you can even stay with the other person (or if your mate will stay with you).

Most likely, the first time you tell your significant other's child to pick something up off the floor, you're going to get the stink-eye from your partner.

Unless there is a threat of harm, disciplining a stepchild will be viewed as out of bounds by most primary parents. In most cases, you will be best served to leave it to them. I know this is particularly hard if a stepparent and spouse have different parenting styles. But if the stepparent takes matters into their own hands directly with the child, they're asking for trouble.

If a stepparent disciplines a stepchild, some parents will blow up at them, maybe even in front of the kids. This will severely undercut the stepparent's authority going forward—something that could come back to haunt everyone later when the stakes are high. If you are a stepparent who this happens to, first, take a deep breath. Then take the opportunity to discuss the matter with the primary parent at a calmer time when the two of you are alone.

Treating Stepchildren Differently Than One's Own Children

This is a tough one for a lot of people and the stereotypical behavior exhibited by that evil stepmom in *Cinderella*. Is it just human nature—a survival instinct—to give the advantage to our own offspring? Or is it because the stepparent and stepchild have not developed a connection?

Whatever it is, many parents fail to treat stepchildren as well as they do their own kids. This can be hurtful to the stepchildren and their primary parent who observes it.

If you are a stepparent unsure if you are treating your stepchildren as well as your own kids, ask your new spouse what he or she thinks. But be prepared to take their criticism. Don't get defensive. You can also ask the kids directly.

Children are usually brutally honest with us—particularly when they are younger. You can even ask your kids, who may feel more comfortable being direct with you than your stepchildren.

If you are an ex-spouse concerned about differences in how children are being treated, share your perception with all the parents involved, being sure to name it as such. For example, say something like, "It may just be how I see it, but I feel like the rules are different from one kid to another. What do you think?" Get the conversation going. Seek to understand the reality and then if warranted, make suggestions on how to make things more equitable for all children.

Expecting Stepparents to Stay Out of Co-parenting Matters

While it's reasonable to ask a stepparent to leave most of the disciplining of your kids to you, you can't expect them to stay out of everything kid-related—especially if the kids spend time in their home.

Remember, it's the stepparent's home too. They should have a say in what goes on there. Plus, they probably care about your kids, want a relationship with them, and want to support them.

The stepparent and primary parent should both compromise on parenting style and choices. If both of you have children, discuss the rules you each expect to maintain. Then work to be as consistent with all kids as possible. Share this information with your co-parent, particularly any changes, and explain the rationale behind them.

If your co-parent disagrees with rules the stepparent imposes on their children, acknowledge that it is a change; ask them to accept that the rules may vary a bit from home to home due to differences in those who live there.

Criticizing Stepchildren

No one wants to be told "your baby is ugly." Parents like to brag about their kids. Some also have great difficulty acknowledging their children's faults. If you're a stepparent inclined to criticize your stepchildren, be prepared for backlash from your spouse's ex and maybe from your spouse as well. They will naturally want to defend their offspring. This doesn't mean you are wrong or should be silent.

If you feel you must bring something to the primary parent's attention, do it privately and be careful to focus on the behavior that disturbed you rather than on the child. Explain what's bothering you and what you might like to see changed. If you can't agree on remedies, pick your battles.

Excluding a Stepparent from Family Conversations and Activities

No one likes to be excluded. How do you feel when two people whisper to each other when you're right there? When a primary parent only discusses situations where the kids are involved with the former spouse, whispers to their children in front of the stepparent, or repeatedly talks to them in private, it makes the stepparent feel like an outsider. It also makes them suspicious that you are hiding information from them. And aren't you?

A friend of mine who is a new stepparent shared that her spouse and stepchildren often whisper to one another when she's around rather than just talking at normal volume. It makes her feel very excluded. What are they hiding? She confided in me that she often wonders if they are talking about her.

When you exclude a stepparent from conversations, you're signaling to your kids that they can't trust their stepparent or should exclude them. If you believe you have valid reasons for being secretive with them, you may have relationship issues you should work on.

When you exclude a stepparent from conversations, you're signaling to your kids that they can't trust their stepparent or should exclude them.

When a co-parent, either the ex or the married parent, excludes a stepparent from family activities, they send the message loud and clear that the stepparent is not to be considered a partner in parenting. Why not instead include them and, in so doing, enlist them as an ally in your parenting efforts?

Failing to Encourage a Connection Between a Stepparent and Stepchildren

Just as a parent has a natural inclination to protect their children, a child feels an obligation to stand up for their parents. As a result, they may hesitate to show affection to a person they perceive as competing with their parent. A primary parent can ignore this hesitation, feed it, or put the child at ease by letting them know that they are encouraged to have a good relationship with their stepparent.

If the stepparent and stepchild relationship is not intentionally encouraged by the co-parents, a relationship that may have been highly rewarding to everyone may never be realized.

Allowing or Encouraging Stepchildren to Disparage or Disrespect a Stepparent

An ex-spouse who doesn't get along with a new spouse may snicker when their children say mean things about the stepparent. Some may even chime in with the kids. Others remain silent and just let the kids continue their rant.

If you allow kids to speak badly about a stepparent, you're encouraging the behavior. They may think it makes you happy. If it does, just realize, you're handicapping their stepparent's efforts to be a positive influence on your children.

Insisting Kids Refer to a Stepparent as Mom or Dad

Insisting that the kids refer to a stepparent as Mom, Mommy, Mother, Dad, Daddy, or Father is an overreach. You're basically saying to them, "I'm replacing your other parent." That will likely bother the children as well as your former spouse. Would it bother you? If the children decide to do this on their own, fine. But don't force it or expect it.

Some blended families are beginning to replace the titles of stepmom and stepdad with *Bonus Mom* and *Bonus Dad*. I like these as they put the stepparenting roles in a much more positive light while preserving the titles of Mom and Dad in all their forms for the primary parents. Adding the word "Bonus" conveys that the family members bring something beneficial to the table. Maybe these titles could work for your family.

Dealing with a Bad Stepparent

Unfortunately, some stepparents really are evil. And some simply don't know what they are doing as parents. Still others have no interest in their stepchildren and work to make it unpleasant for the children to spend time at their home in hopes they'll ask not to come.

We dealt early in this chapter with handling this situation if you're the ex-spouse. But if the stepparent is your spouse and you suspect or have been alerted to the fact that they may not be a good stepparent, I would encourage you to pay attention. Observe how your new spouse cares for and interacts with your children. I'm not suggesting you should hover over them, monitor every interaction, or suspect them of any wrongdoing. But you should be attentive to ensure your children are treated respectfully and given proper care by your new spouse. If your new spouse doesn't have kids of their own, they simply may not know what to do in certain circumstances. In essence they have been thrust into a first-time parent role. Ensure you are giving them the proper support to take on this role.

If you observe behaviors that bother you, I'd talk to your spouse about it to find out what their intent was and explain what bothered you about what you saw. You should also check in with your child to determine if what you observed is a regular occurrence which you may have previously missed. Your #1 priority is always protecting your children from harm—physical, mental, and emotional. Don't be so blinded by your love for this new person that you lose sight of that fact. Trust but verify!

TRUE STORY

A friend of mine shared the following story...

I had two sons with my ex. When we split, our oldest wanted to live with me and the youngest wanted to go with his dad. So that is what we did. I had my youngest every other weekend and one evening during my off-week. But because of a vacation, I hadn't seen him for almost a month. When I finally had him again, he wanted tacos for dinner. As he took his first bite, he groaned and held his hand to his cheek and said that his teeth were hurting very badly. He tried to finish his meal but couldn't. I looked at his face and noticed that his cheeks weren't as full as they had been and that he was pale.

I decided to take him to urgent care. The doctor's diagnosis was shocking...malnutrition! He told me that my son's teeth were very loose, a sign of acute gingivitis. On top of all this, he had lost twelve pounds. The doctor asked my son some

187

questions and learned that when he was a little late for dinner, his stepmother wouldn't let him eat. If he was later than his curfew, she made him sleep on their porch. My son was only eleven years old at the time. This horrified me.

The doctor wrote out a report of the diagnosis, including what my son had told him. When the doctor handed me the report, he told me to get custody of my son as soon as possible, agreeing to testify on my behalf.

I called my lawyer and was awarded a temporary custody order by that Friday, which was my weekend. My son never went back to his father's custody. I was granted full custody two months later. My ex-husband and his wife were only allowed supervised visits with both of the boys after that.

The preceding story demonstrates the need for parents to remain vigilant when their child is spending substantial time in a second home. And your best shot at doing that is to communicate regularly with your co-parent and any other adults caring for your child. But while the above scenario is an extreme example of child abuse, most combative behaviors within blended families are more subtle. However, they can still destroy trust between co-parents.

COLLABORATIVE APPROACH

For the former spouse

- **DO** deal with feelings of jealousy toward a stepparent.
- **DO** give the stepparent a chance. View them as a potential ally in your parenting efforts. Get to know them.
- **DON'T** exclude the stepparent from parenting matters involving your kids. This only makes it more difficult for all of the parents involved to do their best as parents.
- **DON'T** bad-mouth a stepparent to your kids

For the co-parent who has remarried

- **DO** encourage the stepparent and child to spend time together without others. This will help them get to know one another better and provide them an opportunity to bond.
- **DO** share information about your kids with their stepparents—what they have going on, any health concerns, what they struggle with and excel at.
- **DO** invite your former partner and new spouse to get to know one another. Do something social together without the kids to bond as adults.
- **DO** reassure your former spouse that your co-parenting relationship is secure and that you have your children's best interest at heart. If you feel the need, ask them to support your happiness and trust that you will make sure your children are safe and treated fairly. Then ask them to refrain from talking badly about your new spouse—particularly to your kids.
- **DO** question criticism your co-parent wages against your new partner. Remember who you are with now. If concerns are raised by a former spouse, listen, assess the validity of their concerns, and address any real issues. Disregard the rest.
- **DON'T** expect your new spouse to stay out of all matters with your children. You invited them into the family. You are sharing a home. Work it out.
- **DON'T** be secretive around the stepparent. **DON'T** whisper to your kids in front of your new spouse or always leave the room to talk to the kids.

For the stepparent

- **DO** put in the effort to get to know your stepchildren. Attend their games. Go to their concerts. Show them you care and are there to support them. If you didn't want to do these things, you probably shouldn't have joined the family.

- **DON'T** discipline your stepchildren except in matters of safety. Leave this to the parents.
- **DO** discuss both matters of discipline and criticism of the children privately with your spouse. Start by reassuring them that you care for their kids and want the best for them. Then being careful to focus on the behavior that disturbed you rather than on the child, gently explain to them what happened, why it bothered you, and what you might like to see happen. If you disagree on remedies, pick your battles and remember they are their kids first, your stepchildren second. Be careful not to metaphorically tell them that their baby is ugly.
- **DO** recognize that you are the new *kid* on the block and that you may pose a threat to others until they get to know and trust you.
- **DO** speak up to a spouse privately if you feel their children are infringing on your happiness because of either how the kids are acting or how your spouse is treating you in relation to them. Otherwise, resentment will grow and next thing you know, you're deciding if it's all worth it.

For all parents involved

- **DON'T** treat children and stepchildren differently. This is sure to sow resentment. It also won't make you very popular with whomever you're not favoring.
- **DON'T** talk badly about any of the parents or stepparents to the kids. And **DON'T** allow the kids to do it either.
- **DO** remember you're all on the same team as far as the kids are concerned. You are NOT competitors!
- **DO** have realistic expectations. It will take time. You will

not agree on everything. You may like some things about each other and dislike other things. This is no different than any other relationship in your life. Don't expect perfection from anyone or any relationship. Be patient and be prepared to compromise.

THE CO-PARENTING CODE

- **For the former spouse:** Do you want your children to live in a stable and loving home? Are you behaving in a manner that supports that goal? Have you gotten to know the stepparent? Have you given them a fair shake? Can you become comfortable with another person influencing your children? If not, are you seeking help to get there? Do you trust your co-parent's judgment when it comes to parenting and picking people that can be trusted with your kids? They did pick you, after all.

- **For the stepparent:** Are you respecting the primary parents' roles? Are you reassuring them that you support them? Are you acting accordingly? Are you putting in the effort to support the kids and get to know them?

- **For the co-parent who has remarried:** Are you affording your partner your trust and support? Are you doing everything you can to help them form positive relationships with your kids? Are you being forthcoming about information concerning your kids? Do you recognize their right to have a say and influence your kids?

- **For ALL parents and stepparents:** Are you rooting for each other's happiness and helping each other to effectively parent? Do you see yourselves as part of a parenting team?

Notes

STAGE THREE

CORRECTING COURSE

20

CORRECTING COURSE IS ALWAYS POSSIBLE

· · ·

Maybe you got off to a rocky start as co-parents. Maybe things were going well and then somewhere along the way went off the rails. Or maybe you've both thrust so much animosity at each other, you feel the damage is too great for things to ever turn around.

Then again, maybe you and your co-parent are fine but the relationship between you and the new spouse or extended family is a nightmare.

You might have just conceded that this is your life and you're going to have to deal with it. You've tried to be collaborative, but it just hasn't worked. It is hard to keep trying to be nice when all you get in return is anger, hurt, and disappointment.

However, I implore you to never lose hope. I know firsthand that relationships can be repaired—even after a long time has passed. And while I may sound like a broken record at this point, you got it, I'm here to tell you that the best way to do that is by way of the Golden Rule.

COMBATIVE APPROACH

Let's take a look at behaviors that frequently trap two people into a combative stance and derail co-parenting efforts. There are others but the ones I've listed here are the most common that I've seen.

Having an Intense Dislike for Your Co-Parent

One or both parents can't get past their anger or disdain for each other to clear the way for collaboration as parents.

Many couples break up because of horrible things they did to each other. Adultery, emotional abuse, and abandonment are three common scenarios that breed intense animosity toward a former partner. Another is simply growing to dislike each other. Whether you dislike your co-parent or are the one who is disliked in the scenario, you may feel that there is no way you two can ever effectively co-parent. After all, one of you can't even stand to look at the other, much less talk amicably to them.

Something that people often ask me is, how do you get past all that hurt that led to the divorce in the first place so that you can be good parents together? This is probably the most challenging problem to overcome as co-parents. But I have a question for you. Why do you need to? The answer to the question is abundantly simple. Stop trying to fix your problems as a couple. It's over. Whatever happened, happened, and cannot be undone. You've decided to move on from your romantic relationship. But you cannot move on from being parents. Resolving your issues with one another is not a prerequisite for either of you being a good parent. Let it go and move on.

Failing to Apologize for Mistakes

A parent makes a mistake along the way and the co-parenting relationship is damaged. But to make it worse, they don't apologize. Before we write this person off, let's recognize that no one is perfect. We all screw up at some point. Some people have a hard time admitting fault. They may fear the consequences of admitting guilt to a co-parent. They could even be downright embarrassed by their own behavior.

Unfortunately, too many parents don't work past mistakes to recover their co-parenting relationships. In these cases, the opportunity is lost to teach a child about redemption and second chances. Do you believe in these concepts?

Refusing to Forgive Past Misdeeds

Some who messed up their marriages and significant relationships are well aware of what they did wrong. They feel incredible guilt and immense remorse. They just want to turn back time and try to go a different route. But the past is the past and we can't change it. They attempt to apologize but the other co-parent simply won't accept it. They don't feel they owe this now former lover anything, particularly not to be let off the hook for what they did.

Then there are those that may start on a good path. But somewhere along the way, one hurts the other's feelings or does something that the other parent can't believe they did. They refuse to forgive them and constantly throw the past misdeed up as a reason for ceasing to cooperate. Part of it is a self-defense mechanism as they want to prevent the same bad thing from happening again. So, they don't allow things to be reset.

Refusing to Collaborate

One parent tries to collaborate but the other refuses and everyone gives up. Trying to collaborate with an unwilling participant can be extremely frustrating. You're doing all the right things. You know it's best for your child. But your co-parent just won't play along.

Trying to collaborate with an unwilling participant can be extremely frustrating.

At some point, you succumb to failure and give up on the whole idea. You stop treating your co-parent as you want to be treated and instead turn to treating them as you feel *they deserve* to be treated. You accept your fate of having to apologize to your child throughout the rest of their life for your inability to get along as parents for their sake.

TRUE STORY

When I began writing my first book on the topic of co-parenting, I approached my son's father to see if he might want to be involved in the project. Based on my description of the way I planned to organize the book, he thought it sounded like a great idea and agreed to work with me on it.

That first book, *Happily Divorced*, is our story—the story of how Teresa and Bob co-parented their son Ian. I began writing and sending Bob chapters as I completed them. Things went well for the first couple chapters. Then I sent him the chapter that dealt with some of the reasons we decided to divorce. After he got that chapter, things went downhill rapidly.

It turned out he had a vastly different take on these events. He told me he had changed his mind about the book and asked me to stop writing it. Stop? I was all in on this project. How could he ask me to just stop? I suggested he take a break from reading it for a bit. I wrote one or two more chapters and then I did stop or at least paused. I had to step back and consider the consequences of my actions and our co-parenting relationship. The book could NOT kill it!

One day after a full eight months had passed, I was trying to figure out what I should do about the book. I thought about how we had survived and thrived as co-parents and now friends for over twenty years by making sure to consider the other person, by being able to put ourselves in their shoes and live by the Golden Rule. Ah ha! There's the answer. I had to read the book as if I were Bob and see how it struck me.

I started reading my book and everywhere I referred to Bob I thought to myself, how would I feel if someone wrote that about me? It was enlightening. As a result of that exercise, I decided to totally rewrite significant portions of the book.

When I was done rewriting, I asked Bob to please read it. I invited him to highlight anything in the book that still bothered him so that we could discuss it. Later that evening I got a text message from Bob saying he was nine chapters in and so far, had not found the need to highlight anything. Then he called me. We talked for quite a while. He congratulated me on the successful rewrite and wished me well with it. What do you know? The Golden Rule had again enabled our co-parenting relationship to succeed.

COLLABORATIVE APPROACH

All of the combative behaviors listed earlier have two things in common.

1. The behaviors that stand between the two being able to collaborate have all happened in the past. It may be the distant or recent past. But it definitely already happened. There may be an assumption but there is no guarantee that the bad behaviors will ever happen again.

2. At least one person is "choosing" to remain in misery rather than moving out of it. They are either refusing to apologize, refusing to forgive, refusing to try, or refusing to release the past.

Great! We only have two problems to tackle. And the first really isn't a problem since it's already over and done with. Whatever happened may have been awful and inflicted terrible suffering. It may have been yesterday! In fact, you may still be dealing with the consequences of bad behavior that took place in the past. But whatever happened, it is already done and cannot be undone. Can you make it worse? Sure. But whether you do depends entirely on your future decisions. You could also make it better.

DO Accept that Past Events Cannot Be Changed

You can declare it out loud, write it in a journal, tell friends or family, or just affirm it to yourself. It may sound silly. But these intentional acts can help your conscience firmly adopt a new belief as true. Past events cannot be erased or undone!

DO Apologize If You Know You Screwed Up

Whether it is something that happened while you were a couple or since you've been co-parenting, apologize if you know you screwed up. You can apologize face-to-face, which is probably the most meaningful but also the scariest choice. You can apologize by email. You can send a gift to your co-parent asking them to forgive you. It doesn't really matter how you apologize as long as you don't do three things:

DON'T Pair an Apology with an Excuse

When you pair an apology with an excuse, explanation, or justification, no one takes that as a sincere apology. All you're doing is seeking to turn whatever you did from a bad thing into a good thing. Even if you think you had good reasons for doing what you did, you have to be careful in how you word such a message.

For instance, if your co-parent's feelings were hurt by something you said because they misinterpreted you, don't say, "I'm sorry you took it that way, but..."

Instead, try, "I'm sorry that your feelings were hurt by what I said. I assure you that is not what I intended." See, you didn't even admit that *you* hurt their feelings. In fact, no one can hurt anyone else's feelings. We only choose to allow ourselves to be hurt by another's words. So you can say you're sorry without having to admit to something you don't feel you did wrong.

DO Acknowledge the Other Parent's View—Even If You Think It Is Flawed

This doesn't mean you agree with it. It just means you're listening. Say, "I can see why you might have thought that is what I meant." Or even less admitting, "I understand that is how it sounded to you." And by the way, be mindful of your tone on that last option. It could easily turn to sarcasm.

DO Forgive Past Misdeeds

I'm not asking you to forget them. Forgiving someone for a mistake does not erase the mistake for anyone. The immediate consequences have already been realized. If you seek to inflict more cost on your co-parent for past misdeeds, you're now not only hurting them, but you are also hurting yourself and your child.

When you and your co-parent fail at collaborating, your child pays the biggest cost...every time!

Even if the other person doesn't ask to be forgiven, forgive them anyway. Why? Because the act of forgiveness is as much about unburdening them from guilt as it is about freeing you from the heavy weight endured as you carry around that load of anger.

DO Release the Need to Fix Your Relationship with Your Ex

That's right. Just LET IT GO! Release the need to either undo past problems or fix your relationship with your ex. What?!?! That's it? That's my stellar advice for you? Yes, yes it is.

Parents ask me all the time how they can get past the anger to be collaborative. My question is, why do you need to get past it before you can be collaborative? You've already conceded the relationship by splitting up. If you keep insisting that liking them, forgiving them, or hearing an apology from them is a prerequisite to positively co-parent together, you're imposing an unnecessary requirement. Sure, it would be ideal, but your efforts are misplaced. The priority now is on being good parents—not on the two of you fixing your conflicts with one another.

I know that sounds easier said than done. But if you can't forgive your co-parent and/or they won't apologize, just stop focusing on it. Stop burning energy on something you two have already decided not to fix.

We cannot change the past. Nor can we change people. They can only choose to change themselves. For example, if you cheated on them or they on you, neither of you can undo that. You can only build a new kind of relationship going forward. The same is true for every other transgression. They're done!

Instead, accept that things happened and that your romantic relationship is over. Focus on your relationship as co-parents and what you want that to look like for your children.

If you're the culprit, suspend any expectations you have of your co-parent forgiving you. If you were the one wronged, stop waiting for an apology or for your anger to pass before moving forward as a collaborative co-parent. These things don't need to happen first unless you require them to. You just need to focus on being a good parent and enabling your co-parent to be the best parent they can be by collaborating with them.

DO Accept Your Co-parent for Who They Are

If they are irresponsible by nature, don't expect that to change after you separate from them. Find ways to make it easier for them to take responsibility. Why is this your job? Because it is what is required to do the best for your child. How can you help them take responsibility? Here are just a few ideas:

- Create a shared calendar using Google, a co-parenting app, Outlook, or some other software.
- Remind them via text, email, or phone call about their responsibilities, such as picking up a child, dropping them off, attending a game, or joining you for a parent-teacher conference.
- Push back on excuses from your co-parent. Don't let your co-parent out of their responsibilities. If you want to spend more time with your child, this can be hard to do. But I assure you that encouraging the other parent to remain engaged will be better for everyone in the long run.
- Ask them to help you do things for your child— for example, plan and hold a birthday party, build a playhouse, pick out a special type of gift that includes research online, help with physical therapy they are required to do, etc. Keep it manageable—start by giving them small tasks. Provide a lot of detail. Give them a deadline and follow up to ask them how they are doing with the tasks. If they do everything they are supposed

COMBATIVE TO COLLABORATIVE

to, thank them for their help and let them know how important it was to their child's enjoyment of the event.

If they are a workaholic, this is just another form of parental irresponsibility. Use the above strategies to address the workaholic co-parent.

If your co-parent is an alcoholic, drug addict, or suffers from mental issues, you should engage the help of professionals for yourself and your child. You should also do what you can to encourage your ex to get help as well. You may have to seek legal help to keep your child out of harm's way.

THE CO-PARENTING CODE

• • •

As long as both people are living, it's never too late to recover a relationship. It doesn't matter what has happened between the two of you. You can seek redemption or extend multiple chances to a co-parent in the pursuit of a worthy cause—your children. Release the past, focus on the present, and plan for your future.

It's an interesting thing that happens once you release expectations placed on yourself and others. Once the burden of these expectations is removed, you'll often see the behaviors emerge that you wanted all along. It's like when you tell someone not to do some-thing and they dig in their heels and do it anyway. However, if you instead demonstrate the behaviors you want another person to model, they reciprocate.

As you work to correct course in your co-parenting relationships, contemplate the following questions.

- Can you accept that things in the past cannot be changed?
- Have you made fixing your relationship with your ex a prerequisite to collaboratively co-parenting with them?

- Are you withholding a deserved apology out of pride, guilt, or embarrassment?
- Are you refusing to collaborate until you get an apology or until your co-parent (or anyone else for that matter) changes their behavior?
- Are you being combative with your co-parent to make them pay a price for what they did to you? Is this helping your child in any way?
- Can you acknowledge the other person's view even if you disagree with it?
- Can you release hurt and anger without first fixing it?

Notes

ACKNOWLEDGMENTS

Thanks to the many who contributed to the production of this book including editors Ellen Coleman and Rachel Shuster, cover designer, Kay Collins, interior designer Thomas Nery, and author/photographer Kiki Israel. Thanks also to the many parents who provided me with examples of both combative and collaborative co-parenting to share in this book.

Thank you to my mom and dad, Helen and Don Neuhart, who in-stilled in me the principle upon which my entire manner of inter-acting with others is built—the Golden Rule: "Treat others the way you want to be treated."

Special recognition to Brian, Brandi, Michelle, Parker, Madison, and Gracie for being the *bonuses* in our blended/modern family story.

Bob, I pray that our lessons as co-parents will help many. Thank you for helping me to learn them. To Bob's family, I love and cherish all of you.

To my son, Ian, whose beautiful soul, tremendous talent, and extraordinary creativity bring me joy and pride every day. Love you, son!

ABOUT THE AUTHOR

Teresa Harlow is an author and speaker who presents to groups of all kinds on how to transform their most combative relationships into collaborative ones—from that of a former spouse, to a co-worker, child, parent, or even an adversary. To book Teresa to speak, go to her website **www.teresaharlow.com** and submit the online contact form. You may also send an email to info@TeresaHarlow.com.

Discounts are available for bulk book orders. Please email info@PrometheanPublishing.com with your order specifications.

For more co-parenting help, go to **CoparentingCode.com.** Teresa's mission is to take positive co-parenting from being an exception to being the expectation for all divorced parents, their kids, and their loved ones.

Notes

Made in the USA
Las Vegas, NV
30 October 2022

58446217R00122